A CourseGuide for

A Survey of the Old Testament

Andrew E. Hill
John H. Walton

ZONDERVAN ACADEMIC

A CourseGuide for A Survey of the Old Testament

Copyright © 2019 by Andrew E. Hill and John H. Walton

ISBN 978-0-310-11068-2 (softcover)

Requests for information should be addressed to:
Zondervan, 3900 Sparks Dr. SE, Grand Rapids, Michigan 49546

All Scripture quotations, unless otherwise indicated, are taken from The Holy Bible, New International Version®, NIV®. Copyright © 1973, 1978, 1984, 2011 by Biblica, Inc.® Used by permission of Zondervan. All rights reserved worldwide. www.Zondervan.com. The "NIV" and "New International Version" are trademarks registered in the United States Patent and Trademark Office by Biblica, Inc.®

Any internet addresses (websites, blogs, etc.) and telephone numbers in this book are offered as a resource. They are not intended in any way to be or imply an endorsement by Zondervan, nor does Zondervan vouch for the content of these sites and numbers for the life of this book.

No part of this publication may be reproduced, stored in a retrieval system, or transmitted in any form or by any means—electronic, mechanical, photocopy, recording, or any other—except for brief quotations in printed reviews, without the prior permission of the publisher.

Printed in the United States of America

CONTENTS

Introduction 5
1. Approaching the Old Testament 7
2. Geography of the Old Testament 9
3. Introduction to the Pentateuch 12
4. Genesis 15
5. Exodus 18
6. Leviticus 21
7. Numbers 24
8. Deuteronomy 27
9. Historical Overview of the Old Testament Times 30
10. Introduction to the Historical Books 31
11. Joshua 36
12. Judges 39
13. Ruth 42
14. 1-2 Samuel 45
15. 1-2 Kings 48
16. 1-2 Chronicles 51
17. Ezra-Nehemiah 54
18. Esther 57
19. Archaeology and the Old Testament 60
20. Hebrew Poetic and Wisdom Literatuer 63
21. Job 66

22.	Psalms	69
23.	Proverbs	72
24.	Ecclesiastes	75
25.	Song of Songs	78
26.	Formation of the Old Testament Scriptures	81
27.	Introduction to Prophetic Literature	84
28.	Isaiah	87
29.	Jeremiah	90
30.	Lamentations	93
31.	Ezekiel	96
32.	Daniel	99
33.	Hosea	102
34.	Joel	105
35.	Amos	108
36.	Obadiah	111
37.	Jonah	114
38.	Micah	117
39.	Nahum	120
40.	Habakkuk	123
41.	Zephaniah	126
42.	Haggai	129
43.	Zechariah	132
44.	Malachi	135
45.	What We Have Learned	138
46.	Responding to God	140
47.	The Journey to Jesus	142

Introduction

Welcome to *A CourseGuide for A Survey of the Old Testament*. These guides were created for formal and informal students alike who want to engage deeper in biblical, theological, or ministry studies. We hope this guide will provide an opportunity for you to grow not only in your understanding, but also in your faith.

How to Use this Guide

This guide is meant to be used in conjunction with the book *A Survey of the Old Testament* and its corresponding videos, *A Survey of the Old Testament Video Lectures*. After you have read each chapter in the book and watched the accompanying video lesson, the materials in this guide will help you review and assess what you have learned. Application-oriented questions are included as well. For additional practice, you will want to complete exercises found in *A Survey of the Old Testament Workbook*.

Each CourseGuide has been individually designed to best equip you in your studies, but in general, you can expect the following components. Most CourseGuides begin every chapter with a "You Should Know" section, which highlights key terminology, people, and facts to remember. This section serves as a helpful summary for directing your studies. Reflection questions, typically two to three per chapter, prompt you to summarize key points you've learned. Discussion questions invite you to an even deeper level of engagement. Finally, most chapters will end with a short quiz to test your retention. You can find the answer key to each quiz at the bottom of the page following it.

For Further Study

CourseGuides accompany books and videos from some of the world's top biblical and theological scholars. They may be used independently, or in small groups or classrooms, offering quality instruction to equip students for academic and ministry pursuits. If you would like to engage in further study with Zondervan's CourseGuides, the full lineup may be viewed online. After completing your studies with *A CourseGuide for A Survey of the Old Testament*, we recommend moving on to *A CourseGuide for A Survey of the New Testament*, *A CourseGuide for How to Read the Bible for All Its Worth*, and *A CourseGuide for Know How We Got Our Bible*.

CHAPTER 1

Approaching the Old Testament

You Should Know

- Self-revelation: God's revelation of himself to humanity
- The plan: seven-stage process of God's presence among his people
- Covenant: the means by which God reveals himself to, initiates relationship with, and establishes his presence among humanity by entering into a mutually binding agreement with a person or people
- Authority: inherent power of the biblical text over humanity due to its nature as God's self-revelation
- Storyline: the factual content of the text
- Plotline: the theology and substance of the text
- The Old Testament is God's self-revelation to humanity. As such, readers must recognize its authoritative nature and seek to understand as more than literature alone.
- God's plan has always been to exist in relationship with his people. The Bible describes this plan in the seven stages of God's presence: Eden; Covenant; Exodus (Bush/Sinai); Tabernacle/Temple; Incarnation (Immanuel); Pentecost; New Creation.
- In order to understand the Old Testament, readers must distinguish between its storyline, or factual details, and its plotline, or theology and substance.

- Properly applying the Old Testament requires that students understand the original author's intent, which can be accomplished by determining the text's genre, audience, and purpose.

Reflection Questions

1. What are the basic steps involved in interpreting the Old Testament?

2. What is the relationship between the concepts of self-revelation and authority? How do they impact how we study the Old Testament?

Quiz

1. (T/F) Covenant is one of the core concepts of the Old Testament.

2. (T/F) Without realizing it we bring the cultural and historical framework of our own world to the text of the Old Testament.

3. (T/F) One principle of biblical interpretation is that we must speak for the Bible.

4. (T/F) If God is not understood to be the source of the Old Testament, it cannot serve as a *self*-revelation.

5. (T/F) The application of a given Old Testament text should come from an aggregate of impressions gained from reading the text.

6. (T/F) In reading the Old Testament, we should be concerned only with its factual details.

7. (T/F) Readers should try to identify the purpose of the author or editor of the text.

8. (T/F) Eden can be understood as a cosmic temple.

9. (T/F) There are 11 stages of God's presence communicated in the Bible.

10. (T/F) The Old Testament is primarily about God.

ANSWER KEY

1. T, 2. T, 3. F, 4. T, 5. F, 6. F, 7. T, 8. T, 9. F, 10. T

CHAPTER 2

Geography of the Old Testament

You Should Know

- Fertile Crescent: region including the Nile River valley and delta, the plains of Syro-Palestine by the Mediterranean, and the river valleys of the Tigris and Euphrates. Here, the earliest civilizations of the ancient Near East (ANE) developed.

- Mesopotamia: the land between the Tigris and Euphrates rivers

- Levant: lands located along the 400-mile stretch of the Eastern Mediterranean between Turkey and Egypt (including modern-day Syria, Lebanon, and Israel)

- Baal: the Canaanite storm god, deity of agriculture and reproductive fertility

- Oracle: an authoritative prophetic speech

- Syncretism: the combination of different forms of religious belief and practice

- Elect: the choice of the people of Israel (through Abraham) to be God's covenant people

- The nation of Israel developed in a specific geographic context; through the importance of geography in the OT narratives, we see that the Bible records real events taking place in time and space. Our study of geography enriches our understanding of the OT.

- The geography of the ANE immensely influenced Israelite history and culture as Israel interacted with the people groups of the region.

- The land of Canaan was of immense theological significance for the people of Israel, constituting the goal of and reward for obedience to the covenant stipulations.

Reflection Questions

1. What is the theological importance of the land?

2. How might you describe the concept of God as a rock or refuge to a person who had never seen mountains?

Quiz

1. The name "Mesopotamia" means _____.
   a) The city by the river
   b) The land of fertility
   c) The land between the rivers
   d) The land beneath sun

2. Which of the following was NOT a major geographical area in the land of Palestine?
   a) The Coastal Plain
   b) The Southern Highlands
   c) The Central Hill Country
   d) The Transjordan Plateau

3. The region of Syro-Palestine, or the Levant, was a land bridge between _____.
   a) Africa and Asia
   b) Asia and Europe
   c) Europe and Africa
   d) None of the above

4. What is the dominant environmental feature of the Arabian Peninsula?
   a) Forests
   b) Marshlands

c) Rivers
   d) Desert

5. Asia Minor was the home of what powerful empire in the second millennium BC?

   a) Hittites
   b) Ammonites
   c) Assyrians
   d) Edomites

6. Asia Minor is located _____ of the Fertile Crescent.

   a) Northwest
   b) South
   c) East
   d) West

7. Ancient Egypt was divided into how many kingdoms?

   a) One
   b) Two
   c) Three
   d) Four

8. _____ is often called the theological and geographical center of the world.

   a) Palestine
   b) Egypt
   c) Mesopotamia
   d) Anatolia

9. The Moabites and Ammonites traced their lineage to _____.

   a) Abraham
   b) Isaac
   c) Jacob
   d) Lot

10. (T/F) The land of Palestine bears no theological significance.

ANSWER KEY

1. C, 2. B, 3. A, 4. D, 5. A, 6. A, 7. B, 8. A, 9. D, 10. F

CHAPTER 3

Introduction to the Pentateuch

You Should Know

- Pentateuch: Greek expression meaning "five scrolls," consisting of the first five books of the OT: Genesis, Exodus, Leviticus, Numbers, and Deuteronomy

- Torah: a Hebrew term meaning "instruction" in holiness, used by the Jewish community to refer to the first five books of the OT

- Suzerain: a superior feudal ruler; an overlord

- Vassal: a subordinate nation or people group (usually as a result of a treaty following conquest)

- Literary criticism: an interpretive method emphasizing the author's style, literary features, themes, and structure as keys to understanding a biblical text

- Tradition history: an interpretive approach that focuses on the history of the transmission of the biblical traditions by studying the oral traditions during the period of their transmission, and by tracing the development of the written biblical documents, giving special attention to the theological emphases of the community editing and shaping those materials

- Covenant theology: a theological system that understands God's relationship to humanity as a divinely established compact or covenant based on the analogy of the interrelationship of the three persons of the Trinity

- The Pentateuch is unified by the theological theme of the Abrahamic covenant.
- The Pentateuch is composed of diverse literary types and distinctive literary features.
- Though there are undeniable distinctions between the Old and New Testaments, the theological principles that undergird OT law remain intact.

Reflection Questions

1. Describe and differentiate between the five subcategories of legal material found in the OT.

2. Give an overview of each of the two parts of the Pentateuch.

Quiz

1. The use of the name _____ for the first five books of the Old Testament was popularized by Hellenized Jews.

    a) Pentateuch
    b) Decalogue
    c) Pentalogue
    d) The Five

2. Which of the following is NOT an interpretive approach to the NT understanding of the law?

    a) Typological
    b) Allegorical
    c) Fundamental
    d) Didactic

3. Which genre of literature is NOT featured in the first five books of the Old Testament?

    a) Law
    b) Ancient poetry
    c) Epistolatory letter
    d) Narrative prose

4. The Hebrew word for "the Law" is _____.
   a) Gal
   b) Torah
   c) Gorat
   d) Tune

5. Who was the first-century Gnostic heretic who rejected the Old Testament and its "inferior God"?
   a) Malthus
   b) Marcion
   c) Montanus
   d) Martellian

6. Which of the following is NOT a Pentateuchal book?
   a) Genesis
   b) Exodus
   c) Numbers
   d) Judges

7. Which of the following is NOT a subcategory of OT law?
   a) Casuistic law
   b) Apodictic law
   c) The curse
   d) Consternation law

8. (T/F) The unifying theological theme of the first five books of the Old Testament is God's covenant promise to Abram.

9. (T/F) In the New Testament interpretation of the Old Testament Law, Jesus entirely dismissed the teachings of the five books of the Law as "legalism."

10. (T/F) The theological principles behind OT law are no longer relevant for Christians.

ANSWER KEY

1. A, 2. C, 3. C, 4. B, 5. B, 6. D, 7. D, 8. T, 9. F, 10. F

CHAPTER 4

Genesis

You Should Know

- Election: in the OT, the predisposition of God that leads him to arbitrarily select/choose the Israelites (through Abraham) to be his covenant people

- Monotheism: generally defined as the worship of one God, this term can also encompass preference for, or worship of, only one God (possibly accompanied by belief in the existence of other deities), or belief in the existence of only one deity

- Sin: a willful violation of God's expressed will

- Origins: concern the beginning of the existence of the universe

- Primeval history: the earliest history of the world recounted in Genesis 1–11

- Pantheon: a divine assembly of gods and goddesses formally recognized by society as participants in the experiences of community life

- Patriarch: one of the primary ancestors of Israel

- God created, and creation was good.

- Disobedience separated people from God.

- God instituted a program of revelation called the covenant.

Reflection Questions

1. Explain the terms covenant and election, including their theological significance for Christians today.

2. What is "sin" in the book of Genesis and how does it relate to the Christian life today?

Quiz

1. _____ is traditionally attributed authorship of Genesis.
    a) Adam
    b) Moses
    c) Enoch
    d) Joshua

2. In the literature of which culture does the earliest known flood story occur?
    a) Babylonian
    b) Acadian
    c) Sumerian
    d) Greek

3. The book of Genesis ends with Joseph in _____.
    a) Egypt
    b) Syria
    c) Babylon
    d) Assyria

4. Abraham was asked to sacrifice his son _____.
    a) Seth
    b) Shem
    c) Judah
    d) Isaac

5. _____ built the ark in the book of Genesis.
    a) Abraham
    b) Isaac
    c) Joseph
    d) Noah

6. Which of the following is NOT a major theme of Genesis?

   a) Sin
   b) Monotheism
   c) The covenant and election
   d) Kingship

7. _____ was the sign given to Abraham to signify his covenant with God.

   a) Long hair
   b) A beard
   c) Circumcision
   d) White garments

8. Which of the following is NOT a Patriarch?

   a) Abraham
   b) Joseph
   c) Jacob
   d) Hezekiah

9. (T/F) The purpose of the book of Genesis is to tell how and why God came to choose Abraham's family to make a covenant with them.

10. (T/F) Covenant is a significant aspect of the book of Genesis.

ANSWER KEY

1. B, 2. C, 3. A, 4. D, 5. D, 6. D, 7. C, 8. D, 9. T, 10. T

CHAPTER 5

Exodus

You Should Know

- Decalogue: the Ten Commandments

- Documentary hypothesis: an approach to the authorship of the Pentateuch associated with source criticism that understands the five books as a patchwork composition of four (or more) literary documents

- Divine oracle formula: introductory statement indicating direct speech from God to a human agent

- Enlightenment: a philosophical movement of the eighteenth century marked by rejection of traditional social, religious, and political ideas and emphasizing rationalism and scientific methods (equated with modernism)

- Exodus: the event in which Yahweh rescued Israel from slavery in Egypt

- Passover: a feast of unleavened bread that signifies the haste with which Israel left Egypt; the Passover event occurred when Yahweh's messenger brought death to the firstborn of all those who did not have blood from a sacrificial lamb smeared on their doorposts

- Yahweh is supreme over pagan deities.

- The exodus is a redemptive event for ancient Israel.

- The Mosaic law is a religious and social charter for Israel.

- The presence of God is symbolized in the tabernacle.

Reflection Questions

1. What is the purpose and message of Exodus?
2. What is the theological significance of the Passover?

Quiz

1. The name "Exodus" is derived from the Greek Old Testament name for the book, which means _____.

    a) Sadness
    b) Slavery
    c) Departure
    d) Wilderness

2. Who is traditionally thought to be the author of the book of Exodus?

    a) Moses
    b) Joseph
    c) Jethro
    d) Miriam

3. At what mountain did God make a covenant with Israel?

    a) Nebo
    b) Hermon
    c) Sinai
    d) Harnath

4. Which of the following was NOT a plague experienced by Egypt?

    a) Locusts
    b) Hail
    c) Darkness
    d) Fire

5. Which of the following is NOT a route that may have been taken by Israel during the exodus?

    a) Northern
    b) Western
    c) Central
    d) Southern

6. Which of the following is a major theme of Exodus?
   a) Moses
   b) Yahweh
   c) Temple
   d) Egyptian power

7. There were _____ plagues in the book of Exodus.
   a) One
   b) Four
   c) Twelve
   d) Ten

8. (T/F) One of the major themes of the book of Exodus is the presence of God.

9. (T/F) God himself inscribed the Ten Commandments on stone tablets.

10. (T/F) Exodus should not be read as part of the Pentateuch.

ANSWER KEY

1. C, 2. A, 3. C, 4. D, 5. B, 6. B, 7. D, 8. T, 9. T, 10. F

CHAPTER 6

Leviticus

You Should Know

- Atonement: to "pay" for sin by means of sacrifice and offering, as a symbol of repentance and confession before God

- Leviticus: pertaining to the Levites

- Documentary hypothesis: an approach to the authorship of the Pentateuch associated with source criticism that understands the five books as a patchwork composition of four (or more) literary documents

- Tent of meeting: tent where Yahweh met with Moses and delivered parts of the book of Leviticus

- Holiness: a term that conveys the idea of separation from the ordinary for service and/or worship to Yahweh

- Sabbath: a day of rest that indicated Israel's special relationship with God and testified that Israel's holiness was rooted in Yahweh, not ritual

- The purity of the covenant community

- The principle of substitution in the sacrificial ritual

- The principle of mediation in the service of the priests

- The redeeming of time by means of the liturgical calendar

Reflection Questions

1. What is the significance of the Levitical sacrificial system for Christians today?

2. What is the significance of the Sabbath for Christians today?

Quiz

1. The book of Leviticus contains instructions for all of the following EXCEPT _____.

    a) Priestly regulations
    b) Parceling out of tribal land
    c) Priestly duties
    d) Practical "holy living"

2. Which of the following was NOT typically offered as a sacrifice in the ancient world?

    a) Animals
    b) Grain
    c) Drinks
    d) Clothing

3. The English name "Leviticus" is derived from the Greek title for the book meaning _____.

    a) Pertaining to the Levites
    b) Sacrifices
    c) Priests
    d) By the Levites

4. All of the following were offerings instituted for Israel in Leviticus EXCEPT _____.

    a) Abundance offerings
    b) Cereal offerings
    c) Peace offerings
    d) Sin offerings

5. Spiritual sacrifices in the New Testament include all of the following EXCEPT _____.

    a) Generous and cheerful giving
    b) Prayer

c) Worship
d) Sunday school attendance

6. How many basic types of sacrifices are there in Leviticus?
   a) One
   b) Two
   c) Five
   d) Ten

7. (T/F) One of the major themes of Leviticus is the holiness of God.

8. (T/F) No other culture in the ancient Near East besides Israel practiced ritual purification.

9. (T/F) The Sabbath showed that Israel's holiness was rooted in the Lord.

10. (T/F) The Old Testament teaches that animal sacrifice was intended to save people from sin.

ANSWER KEY
1. B, 2. D, 3. A, 4. A, 5. D, 6. C, 7. T, 8. F, 9. T, 10. F

CHAPTER 7

Numbers

You Should Know

- Documentary hypothesis: an approach to the authorship of the Pentateuch associated with source criticism that understands the five books as a patchwork composition of four (or more) literary documents

- Kadesh: area where Israel camped after leaving Sinai

- Seer: a technical term applied to certain Old Testament prophets, especially signifying divine revelation received in the form of a dream or vision

- Moab: area where the second generation of Israel camped just before entering Canaan

- Sinai: mountain where the children of Israel camped after leaving Egypt

- Supracultural: divine revelation prohibiting or superseding the cultural norms of the Old Testament world

- God's faithfulness to his covenant promises

- Divine testing of human motives

- God communicating his truth through the medium of culture

- God's sovereign rule of the nations

Reflection Questions

1. What was the purpose of the wilderness wanderings? Was God "fair" in causing the Israelites to wander for forty years?

2. What do the *two* Balaam narratives in Numbers teach about the relationship between divine sovereignty and human responsibility?

Quiz

1. The Hebrew title of the book of Numbers means _____.

    a) In the wilderness
    b) Counting the people
    c) During the census
    d) Wandering

2. Which of the following is NOT a major theme in the book of Numbers?

    a) The census numbers
    b) The revelation of God in human culture
    c) Social justice
    d) The testing by Yahweh

3. How many censuses were recorded in the book of Numbers?

    a) One
    b) Two
    c) Three
    d) Four

4. Which of the following is not a major geographical area in Numbers?

    a) Moab
    b) Sinai
    c) Kadesh
    d) Egypt

5. Who was the pagan prophet who was sent to curse Israel but ended up blessing them instead?

    a) Zophar
    b) Bildad
    c) Tobit
    d) Balaam

6. (T/F) The book of Numbers has nothing to say about Yahweh's covenant faithfulness.

7. (T/F) According to Numbers, Yahweh does not reveal himself to Israel.

8. (T/F) One of the major themes in the book of Numbers is testing by God.

9. (T/F) Numbers records none of Israel's responses to the surrounding culture.

10. (T/F) God never tests his elect.

ANSWER KEY

1. A, 2. C, 3. B, 4. D, 5. D, 6. F, 7. F, 8. T, 9. F, 10. F

CHAPTER 8

Deuteronomy

You Should Know

- Torah: a Hebrew term meaning "instruction" in holiness, used by the Jewish community to refer to the first five books of the OT
- Suzerain: a superior feudal ruler; an overlord
- Vassal: a subordinate nation or people group (usually as a result of a treaty following conquest)
- Monotheism: generally defined as the worship of one God, this term can also encompass preference for, or worship of, only one God (possibly accompanied by belief in the existence of other deities), or belief in the existence of only one deity
- Documentary hypothesis: an approach to the authorship of the Pentateuch associated with source criticism that understands the five books as a patchwork composition of four (or more) literary documents
- The importance of a central worship place
- The emphasis on the name of God
- The organization of laws with reference to the Ten Commandments
- The centrality of loving and obeying the covenant God

Reflection Questions

1. Describe the retribution principle as found in Deuteronomy. Does it apply today? If so, how?

2. What are the major parts of ancient Near Eastern vassal treaties? How does knowing this literary background help you understand Deuteronomy?

Quiz

1. The name "Deuteronomy," from the Greek title for the book, means _____.
    a) Second law
    b) New law
    c) Great law
    d) Lawgiver

2. Which of the following is NOT a major theme in the book of Deuteronomy?
    a) Priestly functions
    b) Central sanctuary
    c) Law
    d) Retribution principle

3. Which of the following is NOT one of the Ten Commandments?
    a) You shall not murder
    b) Honor your father and your mother
    c) You shall not give false testimony against your neighbor
    d) You shall not trespass

4. _____ is an ancient collection of Mesopotamian laws.
    a) Hammurabi's Stele
    b) The Annals of Ashurbanipal
    c) The Eliphaz Codex
    d) Shammai's Tablet

5. The Ten Commandments emphasize all of the following EXCEPT _____.
    a) Divine authority
    b) Human superiority

    c) Divine dignity
    d) Human dignity

6. The retribution principle describes how God operates with _____.

    a) Nations
    b) Individuals
    c) Families
    d) Neighborhoods

7. Who is traditionally considered the author of Deuteronomy?

    a) Hezekiah
    b) Abraham
    c) Moses
    d) Joseph

8. Standard ancient Near Eastern treaties include which of the following?

    a) Preamble
    b) Historical prologue
    c) Stipulations
    d) All of the above

9. (T/F) Deuteronomy teaches a sharp distinction between law and grace.

10. (T/F) The Ten Commandments have no ongoing significance for the Christian.

ANSWER KEY

1. A, 2. A, 3. D, 4. A, 5. B, 6. A, 7. C, 8. D, 9. F, 10. F

CHAPTER 9

Historical Overview of Old Testament Times

You Should Know

- Mesopotamia: the land between the Tigris and Euphrates rivers

- Assyrian Empire: major power in the ancient Near East ca. 1076–612 BC

- Egyptian Empire: major power in the ancient Near East ca. 2000–1200 BC

- Babylonian Empire: major power in the ancient Near East ca. 612–539 BC

- Persian Empire: major power in the ancient Near East ca. 539–332 BC

- Late Bronze Age: period lasting from 1500 to 1200 BC during which major ancient Near Eastern powers were in a constantly fluctuating stalemate

- Iron Age I: period lasting from 1200–1000 BC during which a power vacuum existed in the ancient Near East, allowing for the rise of the Israelite nation

- The establishment of Israel occurred in real time and space.

- Various empires constantly vied for control of the ancient Near East.

- International politics played a significant role in the history of Israel and Judah.

Historical Overview of Old Testament Times | 31

Reflection Questions

1. Why should students of the Bible learn about the historical/cultural context in which it is situated?

2. What led to the downfall and exile of Israel?

Quiz

1. What is the "fixed point" from which the chronology of the Old Testament can be determined?
   a) Conquest lists of the Hittites
   b) Invasion annals of King Nebuchadrezzar
   c) Eponym lists of Assyria
   d) Royal court transcripts of Egypt

2. Which natural phenomenon mentioned in official records helps historians pinpoint a "primary anchor" point in history to determine the absolute chronology of the ancient Near East?
   a) An earthquake
   b) A comet
   c) A solar eclipse
   d) A flood

3. King Josiah of Judah died fighting against _____, while trying to stop their attempt to lend assistance to _____.
   a) Assyria, Babylon
   b) Babylon, Syria
   c) Egypt, Assyria
   d) Syria, Egypt

4. Who were the "architects" for Mesopotamian culture?
   a) Sumerians
   b) Phoenicians
   c) Hittites
   d) Lebanese

5. Who deported Israel?
   a) Judah
   b) Egypt
   c) Assyria
   d) Babylon

6. Who deported Judah?
   a) Judah
   b) Egypt
   c) Assyria
   d) Babylon

7. Under which nation did the Judeans return home after being exiled?
   a) Babylon
   b) Persia
   c) Medo-Persia
   d) Assyria

8. King David ruled Israel during which period of time?
   a) Early Bronze Age
   b) Late Bronze Age
   c) Iron Age I
   d) Patriarchal Period

9. (T/F) The Persian Empire was the last of the great Mesopotamian empires before Alexander the Great and the Greeks conquered all of the "known world."

10. (T/F) Ancient Near Eastern history is unimportant for interpreting the Old Testament.

ANSWER KEY

1. C, 2. C, 3. C, 4. A, 5. C, 6. D, 7. C, 8. C, 9. T, 10. F

CHAPTER 10

Introduction to the Historical Books

You Should Know

- Deuteronomistic school: (hypothetical) Hebrew scribal guild of the seventh century BC responsible for shaping the historical literature of the Old Testament (Deuteronomy–2 Kings)

- Deuteronomistic history: Martin Noth proposed that Deuteronomy–2 Kings is a unified work written primarily during the exilic period. This term describes Deuteronomy–2 Kings in Noth's theory, which remains a dominant theory today.

- Historiography: the writing of history or the product of historical writing; a collection of historical literature

- Historical books: Old Testament books Joshua, Judges, Ruth, 1 and 2 Samuel, 1 and 2 Kings, 1 and 2 Chronicles, Ezra, Nehemiah, and Esther

- Linear model of history: view of history in which history is seen as a straight line moving from the beginning to the end along the continuum of time

- Recurrence model of history: view of history in which there is a fixed sequence of several stages through which history passes, returning eventually to an original point

- The Historical Books comprise Joshua, Judges, Ruth, 1 and 2 Samuel, 1 and 2 Kings, 1 and 2 Chronicles, Ezra, Nehemiah, and Esther.

- The Deuteronomic History, which argues that Deuteronomy–2 Kings are a unified work written during the exile, is the primary framework for most research on the Historical Books.

- People in the ancient Near East and biblical world held to a recurrence model of history rather than a linear model of history.
- The Old Testament recorded history for primarily theological purposes.

Reflection Questions

1. What is the recurrence model of history and how does it differ from the linear model of history?

2. What is the primary purpose of historical literature in the Old Testament? Explain.

Quiz

1. In the Hebrew arrangement of the books of the Old Testament, Joshua, Judges, and the books of Samuel and Kings form a section known as the _____.
    a) Writings
    b) Torah
    c) Former Prophets
    d) Latter Prophets

2. The books of Ruth, Chronicles, Ezra, Nehemiah, and Esther form a section known as the _____.
    a) Writings
    b) Torah
    c) Former Prophets
    d) Latter Prophets

3. Which Old Testament book is often said to have influenced the theology of the books of Joshua-Kings?
    a) Genesis
    b) Exodus

c) Deuteronomy
d) Isaiah

4. The so-called Deuteronomistic History includes all of the following books EXCEPT _____.
   a) Deuteronomy
   b) 2 Kings
   c) Jeremiah
   d) Judges

5. Which scholar is primarily responsible for the theory of the Deuteronomistic History?
   a) Martin Noth
   b) John Walton
   c) Martin Heidegger
   d) Gerhard von Rad

6. Which of the following was viewed as a potential source for omens in the ancient Near East?
   a) The motion of heavenly bodies
   b) Animal entrails
   c) The flight of birds
   d) All of the above

7. (T/F) In the ancient Near East, history was viewed as a linear progression toward an end point.

8. (T/F) Historical documents from the ancient Near East were often propaganda clothed in historical attire.

9. (T/F) The purpose of the Bible's historical literature is to teach about God.

10. (T/F) In order to best interpret the historical books, we should think of them as theological instead of historical.

ANSWER KEY

1. C, 2. A, 3. C, 4. C, 5. A, 6. D, 7. F, 8. T, 9. T, 10. T

CHAPTER 11

Joshua

You Should Know

- Deuteronomistic school: (hypothetical) Hebrew scribal guild of the seventh century BC responsible for shaping the historical literature of the Old Testament (Deuteronomy–2 Kings)
- Ban: in war, to consecrate a city and its inhabitants to destruction; carry out this destruction; totally annihilate a population in war
- Canaan: area of land in Palestine conquered by the Israelites
- Historicity: historical accuracy and truthfulness
- Hyksos: Semitic people group that ruled Egypt ca. 1800 BC until ca. 1650 BC
- Israelite Conquest/conquest: term used to describe Israel's invasion of Canaan and defeat of peoples living there
- Etiological legend: fictional story contrived to explain an observed phenomenon or situation
- The faithfulness of God in fulfilling the covenant promises.
- The conquest and apportionment of the land.
- The importance of obedience.

Reflection Questions

1. What are the major views of the conquest?
2. Why is the book of Joshua so careful to make it clear that God

is responsible for the Israelites' military victories? What are some modern-day implications of this?

Quiz

1. Joshua was all of the following EXCEPT _____

    a) An assistant to Moses
    b) A general
    c) A priest
    d) One of the twelve spies who went into Canaan

2. Which of the following is a reason the authors provide that justifies the ban in Joshua?

    a) The Canaanite economy
    b) God is capricious
    c) Canaanites resisted the Lord
    d) Canaanites worshiped Yahweh

3. Which of the following is a common misconception among Christians about the book of Joshua?

    a) It's only the story of a godly person
    b) It is historically accurate
    c) It recounts Israel's conquest of Canaan
    d) It describes God's strategies for the conquest

4. Which of these is NOT a major theme in the book of Joshua?

    a) Covenant and land
    b) Sovereign involvement
    c) The ban
    d) Need for a king

5. (T/F) The book of Joshua is primarily about Joshua as a courageous, godly leader and about military conquest.

6. (T/F) Possessing land was central to Israel's covenant with God.

7. (T/F) The book of Joshua is an etiological legend.

8. (T/F) During the period of the conquest there was one major power that controlled Palestine.

9. (T/F) In the book of Joshua God is pictured as engaging in combat on Israel's behalf.

10. (T/F) The book of Joshua goes to great lengths to communicate that Yahweh alone deserved credit for Israelite military victories.

ANSWER KEY

1. C, 2. C, 3. A, 4. D, 5. F, 6. T, 7. F, 8. F, 9. T, 10. T

CHAPTER 12

Judges

You Should Know

- Theocracy: a state or nation ruled directly by God
- Canaan: area of land in Palestine conquered by the Israelites
- Deuteronomistic school: (hypothetical) Hebrew scribal guild of the seventh century BC responsible for shaping the historical literature of the Old Testament (Deuteronomy–2 Kings)
- Deuteronomistic history: Martin Noth proposed that Deuteronomy–2 Kings is a unified work written primarily during the exilic period. This term describes Deuteronomy–2 Kings in Noth's theory, which remains a dominant theory today.
- Judge: charismatic leader appointed by God to lead Israel for a specific time and purpose
- The cycle of the judges period
- God's justice and grace
- God's sovereign provision of deliverers
- Covenant failure by the people, the priests, and the tribal leadership
- The role of the Spirit of the Lord

Reflection Questions

1. What is the theological purpose of the book of Judges?

2. Describe the cycle of sin and deliverance in the book of Judges. How does it compare with God's work in the church?

Quiz

1. Which of these is NOT a major theme of the book of Judges?
   a) The nature of charismatic leadership
   b) The Spirit of the Lord
   c) Israel's apostasy
   d) The blessings of the covenant

2. Who of the following people listed was NOT a judge?
   a) Deborah
   b) Samson
   c) Jephthah
   d) Bildad

3. The task of a judge was to be a _____.
   a) Deliverer
   b) Monitor
   c) Civil authority
   d) Spiritual leader

4. Which judge was endowed with the Spirit of the Lord on a number of occasions to accomplish deliverance for God's people?
   a) Ehud
   b) Deborah
   c) Samson
   d) Barak

5. The book of Judges takes place in _____.
   a) Egypt
   b) Babylon
   c) Canaan
   d) Assyria

6. In the book of Judges, the government in Israel is a _____.
   a) Theocracy
   b) Monarchy
   c) Oligarchy
   d) Democracy

7. (T/F) The purpose of the book of Judges was to explore what happened theologically during the years between Joshua and David.

8. (T/F) The phrase "in those days Israel had no king" is repeated often in the book of Judges.

9. (T/F) The people of Israel repeatedly sin against God in the book of Judges.

10. (T/F) The judges are intended to be spiritual examples for Christians to follow.

ANSWER KEY

1. D, 2. D, 3. A, 4. C, 5. C, 6. A, 7. T, 8. T, 9. T, 10. F

CHAPTER 13

Ruth

You Should Know

- Writings: third division of the Jewish canon, in which Ruth is placed
- Historiography: the writing of history or the product of historical writing; a collection of historical literature
- Historical books: Old Testament books Joshua, Judges, Ruth, 1 and 2 Samuel, 1 and 2 Kings, 1 and 2 Chronicles, Ezra, Nehemiah, and Esther
- *Hesed*: Hebrew term that describes God's covenant faithfulness, or loyal love, for his people
- Kinsman-Redeemer: closest living relative to a deceased head of household who redeems land sold or otherwise lost by a relative
- Moabites: people group descended from Lot who were enemies of the Israelites
- God's faithfulness and loyalty stimulated by people's faithfulness and loyalty to one another
- David's faith shown to be the legacy of his ancestors
- The light of loyalty dispersed during the apostasy of the Judges period
- The concept of kinsman-redeemer introduced

Reflection Questions

1. What is a kinsman-redeemer? What is its function in the book of Ruth?

2. What does the word *hesed* mean? What is its theological significance?

Quiz

1. _____ is a major theme in the book of Ruth.
    a) The need to seek wisdom
    b) Hesed
    c) The need to renew temple worship
    d) Boquer

2. Ruth was a member of the nation of _____.
    a) Ammon
    b) Damascus
    c) Edom
    d) Moab

3. Which feature of the book of Ruth suggests it is a product of the monarchy period at the earliest?
    a) The use of the term "kinsman-redeemer"
    b) The closing genealogy
    c) Several Aramaic words
    d) It says that it was written during the monarchy period

4. The Hebrew word *hesed* can be translated by all of the following words EXCEPT _____.
    a) Kindness
    b) Love
    c) Pity
    d) Loyalty

5. Who is a direct descendant of Ruth?
    a) David
    b) Jonathan
    c) Saul
    d) Noah

6. In the Jewish ordering of the OT, Ruth is in the _____.

a) Former Prophets
b) Latter Prophets
c) Pentateuch
d) Writings

7. (T/F) Moabites were welcome in the nation of Israel.

8. (T/F) The book of Ruth is considered part of the Deuteronomistic History.

9. (T/F) The author of the book is identified as Samuel.

10. (T/F) God's covenant loyalty is an important concept in Ruth.

ANSWER KEY

1. B, 2. D, 3. B, 4. C, 5. A, 6. D, 7. F, 8. F, 9. F, 10. T

CHAPTER 14

1–2 Samuel

You Should Know

- Lament: an appeal to a merciful God for divine intervention in a desperate situation

- Monarchy: system of government in which a single ruler (monarch) has complete authority over the affairs of the nation

- Saul: first king of Israel

- David: second king of Israel

- Ark of the covenant: most important religious artifact in Israel, it represented Yahweh's presence

- First and Second Samuel were originally one book which followed Israel's history from the conclusion of the judges period to the establishment of the monarchy.

- The primary purpose of this book is to record the history of the Davidic covenant and also to demonstrate that David did not usurp the throne.

- The institution of kingship

- The process toward establishing a covenant with David's line

- The importance of divine kingship

Reflection Questions

1. Briefly outline the Succession Narrative (2 Samuel 10–20) and give at least two practical applications from these chapters.

2. Compare and contrast the lives of Saul and David.

Quiz

1. Which of the following is NOT a major theme of 1 and 2 Samuel?
   a) The Davidic covenant
   b) Kingship
   c) The ark of the covenant
   d) Reforming temple worship

2. In the books of 1 and 2 Samuel, Samuel functions as a _____.
   a) Prophet, king, and priest
   b) Servant, judge, and priest
   c) King, warrior, and prophet
   d) Prophet, priest, and judge

3. Which of these men was NOT one of Israel's kings?
   a) David
   b) Samuel
   c) Solomon
   d) Saul

4. Who was the first king of Israel?
   a) Saul
   b) Samuel
   c) David
   d) Rehoboam

5. Which is not a reason that David should not be considered a usurper?
   a) Saul's animosity
   b) David's nonaggression
   c) Saul's superb leadership
   d) Presentation of statements that affirm David's innocence

6. In the books of Samuel, the people wanted which form of government to be instituted?

a) Monarchy
b) Oligarchy
c) Democracy
d) Theocracy

7. Which of the following is not a primary character in the books of Samuel?
   a) David
   b) Saul
   c) Samuel
   d) Isaiah

8. (T/F) Saul was generally viewed as a positive king.

9. (T/F) The books of 1 and 2 Samuel originally constituted a single book.

10. (T/F) Though the Davidic covenant is significant in the books of 1 and 2 Samuel, it plays a fairly unimportant role in the rest of the Old Testament.

ANSWER KEY

1. D, 2. D, 3. B, 4. A, 5. C, 6. A, 7. D, 8. F, 9. T, 10. F

CHAPTER 15

1–2 Kings

You Should Know

- Dynastic succession: royal authority legitimized by heredity; rulers come from the same line of descent

- United monarchy: period of time during which Israel and Judah were ruled by the same king

- Divided monarchy: period of time during which Israel and Judah were ruled by different kings

- Osiris: the Egyptian god of the underworld

- The prophetic voice as the royal conscience.

- Covenant blessings (repentance and restoration) and curses (judgment and exile)

- The books of 1 and 2 Kings record the history of Israel from the death of David to the fall of Jerusalem and the end of Hebrew national independence.

- The book surveys the history of Israel from the united empire under Solomon to the split of the monarchy under Rehoboam and records the political and religious occurrences of the divided kingdoms until their end.

- Kings functions as a record of the covenantal failures of the Israelite kings and priests, who led the people into spiritual apostasy.

- The books offer a clear commentary on worship, focusing on Yahwism vs. Baalism.

Reflection Questions

1. Give a brief overview of the monarchy in Israel.

2. Compare and contrast the way that the books of Kings evaluate national leadership with how we evaluate national leadership.

Quiz

1. Which of the following was NOT a major theme in 1 and 2 Kings?
    a) Assessment of King Solomon
    b) Dynastic succession and charismatic leadership
    c) The ark of the covenant
    d) The golden calf cult

2. The city of Jerusalem fell in _____.
    a) 587/586 BC
    b) 722 BC
    c) 971/970 BC
    d) 612 BC

3. Which two prophets functioned in the northern kingdom during the divided monarchy?
    a) Elijah and Elisha
    b) Nathan and Zechariah
    c) Isaiah and Jeremiah
    d) Samuel and Balaam

4. The shrines of the golden calf cult were located at _____.
    a) Dan and Bethel
    b) Shechem and Gilgal
    c) Samaria and Tizrah
    d) Beersheba and Gaza

5. Which prophet rebuked David?
    a) Elijah
    b) Elisha

c) Nathan
   d) Samuel

6. King Solomon was known for all of the following EXCEPT _____.

   a) Ushering in a "golden age"
   b) Immense wealth
   c) Fighting the Philistines and recovering land that was lost
   d) Failure due to seductions of foreign wives

7. Who was the last king of the united monarchy?

   a) Solomon
   b) David
   c) Saul
   d) Rehoboam

8. The golden calf is likely based off of which false god?

   a) Ra
   b) Baal
   c) Osiris
   d) Isis

9. Which of the following policies did NOT contribute to the split of the kingdom?

   a) Political alliance to foreign nations by marriage
   b) Tendencies toward religious syncretism
   c) Proliferation of state bureaucracy
   d) Faithfulness to Yahweh

10. (T/F) The primary purpose of the books of 1 and 2 Kings was to record Israel's continued covenant faithfulness.

ANSWER KEY

1. C, 2. A, 3. A, 4. A, 5. C, 6. C, 7. A, 8. C, 9. D, 10. F

CHAPTER 16

1–2 Chronicles

You Should Know

- **Ahura Mazda:** the supreme being of Persian Zoroastrianism represented as a deity of goodness and light, and whose symbol was fire

- **Colophon:** an addendum or postscript attached to a manuscript, sometimes containing facts relative to its writing

- **Typology:** one aspect of biblical interpretation that establishes a correspondence between Old Testament events, persons, objects, and/or ideas ("types") and their New Testament counterparts ("antetypes") by way of foreshadowing or prototype

- **Libation:** the act of pouring a liquid as a sacrifice to a deity (e.g., upon a stone, Gen. 35:14)

- **Deuteronomistic history:** Martin Noth proposed that Deuteronomy–2 Kings is a unified work written primarily during the exilic period. This term describes Deuteronomy–2 Kings in Noth's theory, which remains a dominant theory today.

- **Historical books:** Old Testament books Joshua, Judges, Ruth, 1 and 2 Samuel, 1 and 2 Kings, 1 and 2 Chronicles, Ezra, Nehemiah, and Esther

- The retelling of the past to inspire hope in the present

- The reigns of David and Solomon idealized

- The centrality of worship

- The validation of the priests and Levites as community leaders

Reflection Questions

1. Describe the concept of typology and its role in the books of Chronicles.

2. In what ways does the chronicler demonstrate the importance of corporate *and* individual responsibility in the books of Chronicles?

Quiz

1. Which of the following is NOT a major theme in Chronicles?
    a) Worship in the Old Testament
    b) Typology
    c) The conquering of the land
    d) The chronicler's vocabulary

2. _____ is portrayed by the chronicler as a "good" king.
    a) Hezekiah
    b) Ahaz
    c) Jehu
    d) Manasseh

3. The chronicler idealized which two kings as the "type figures" of a "good" king?
    a) Saul and Jeroboam
    b) David and Solomon
    c) Hezekiah and Josiah
    d) Ahaziah and David

4. _____ were the equivalent of professional clergy in Israel.
    a) Priests and Levites
    b) Kings
    c) Prophets
    d) Worship leaders

5. The chronicler emphasized the kingship of _____.
    a) Saul
    b) Jeroboam

c) David
d) Rehoboam

6. (T/F) Chronicles concentrates on the legitimization of the priestly and Levitical authority.

7. (T/F) Chronicles shows no concern for the temple or worship.

8. (T/F) The chronicler uses very simple language and syntax leading many scholars to believe he is from humble origins and likely uneducated.

9. (T/F) Typology establishes historical correspondence between the OT and the NT.

10. (T/F) Chronicles focuses on the divided monarchy.

ANSWER KEY

1. C, 2. A, 3. B, 4. A, 5. C, 6. T, 7. F, 8. F, 9. T, 10. F

CHAPTER 17

Ezra–Nehemiah

You Should Know

- Apocrypha: a collection of intertestamental Jewish literature, recognized as deuterocanonical in some Christian traditions

- Hellenism: the influence of Greek thought, language, and culture spread throughout the Near East after the conquests of Alexander the Great

- Deuteronomistic history: Martin Noth proposed that Deuteronomy–2 Kings is a unified work written primarily during the exilic period. This term describes Deuteronomy–2 Kings in Noth's theory, which remains a dominant theory today.

- Historical books: Old Testament books Joshua, Judges, Ruth, 1 and 2 Samuel, 1 and 2 Kings, 1 and 2 Chronicles, Ezra, Nehemiah, and Esther

- Exilic: term describing the period during which both Israel and Judah were exiled from the Promised Land

- Postexilic: term describing the period after which the people of Judah were repatriated by Cyrus

- Ezra and Nehemiah both ministered to Jerusalem during the postexilic period.

- The physical restoration of the city of Jerusalem

- Yahweh as a covenant-keeping God

- Religious and social reform as the aftermath of repentance

Reflection Questions

1. Why was it important theologically and psychologically for the people of Israel to rebuild Jerusalem?

2. Based on Ezra-Nehemiah, what does it mean for Yahweh to be a covenant-keeping God?

Quiz

1. Ezra and Nehemiah came from the Persian city of _____.

    a) Ecbatana
    b) Susa
    c) Persepolis
    d) Babylon

2. Ezra and Nehemiah came to Jerusalem during the reign of King _____.

    a) Darius
    b) Artaxerxes I
    c) Nabopolassar
    d) Ashurbanipal

3. One of the primary genres in Ezra-Nehemiah is _____.

    a) Fiction
    b) Memoir
    c) Fan fiction
    d) Poetry

4. Nehemiah was the cupbearer for which king?

    a) David
    b) Darius
    c) Cyrus
    d) Artaxerxes I

5. Nehemiah undertook an initiative to do what in Jerusalem?

a) Build aqueducts to secure a source of water
b) Reestablish a market for commercial trade
c) Rebuild the walls around Jerusalem
d) Exterminate rats who were causing diseases

6. Reforms instituted by Ezra and Nehemiah addressed all of the following EXCEPT _____.

   a) Intermarriage with foreign women
   b) Social injustice
   c) Improper worship
   d) Failure to circumcise

7. (T/F) One of the dominant theological themes in Ezra-Nehemiah is covenant renewal in the postexilic community.

8. (T/F) The author of Ezra-Nehemiah had a theological purpose in writing the books.

9. (T/F) Ezra and Nehemiah form a single book in the Hebrew Bible.

10. (T/F) The second temple was more magnificent than the first temple built by Solomon.

ANSWER KEY

1. B, 2. B, 3. B, 4. D, 5. C, 6. D, 7. T, 8. T, 9. T, 10. F

CHAPTER 18

Esther

You Should Know

- Deuteronomistic history: Martin Noth proposed that Deuteronomy–2 Kings is a unified work written primarily during the exilic period. This term describes Deuteronomy–2 Kings in Noth's theory, which remains a dominant theory today.
- Historical books: Old Testament books Joshua, Judges, Ruth, 1 and 2 Samuel, 1 and 2 Kings, 1 and 2 Chronicles, Ezra, Nehemiah, and Esther
- Exilic: term describing the period during which both Israel and Judah were exiled from the Promised Land
- Purim: festival that celebrates God's deliverance of Israel as recorded in the book of Esther
- Persian Empire: major power in the ancient Near East ca. 539–332 BC
- Xerxes: King who ruled Persia during the time of Esther
- Conveys a theological message to the scattered Israelites of God's protection of his people and his judgment against their enemies
- God is at work even when he is behind the scenes.
- The schemes of the wicked are doomed.
- God's plan for his people cannot be thwarted.

Reflection Questions

1. Is it significant that Yahweh is not mentioned explicitly in Esther? Explain.

2. Compare and contrast Haman and Mordecai. With whom do you most identify? Why?

Quiz

1. The book of Esther is read annually at the Jewish festival of
_____.

   a) Purim
   b) Yom Kippur
   c) Passover
   d) Hanukkah

2. _____ is the antagonist in the book of Esther who plots to have all of the Jews in Persia killed.

   a) Mordecai
   b) Korah
   c) Haman
   d) Abner

3. What is another name for King Xerxes?

   a) Ahasuerus
   b) Mordecai
   c) Artaxerxes
   d) Hezekiah

4. What is the earliest century to which Hebrew manuscripts of Esther date?

   a) Tenth century AD
   b) Seventh century BC
   c) Eleventh century AD
   d) Seventh century AD

5. Which nation defeated Persia?

   a) Greece
   b) Egypt
   c) Assyria
   d) Babylon

6. Which modern-day genre is Esther most like?

   a) Play
   b) Short story
   c) Novel
   d) Poetry

7. The plotline of Esther revolves around an attempt to _____.

   a) Exile the Jews from Persia
   b) Exterminate the Jews
   c) Assimilate the Jews
   d) Make the Jews wealthy

8. (T/F) The author of the book of Esther demonstrates an extensive knowledge of the operation of the Persian court.

9. (T/F) Esther is the only book in the Bible which does not mention the name of God.

10. (T/F) The prophetic theme of God's protection of his people can be seen in the plot of Esther.

ANSWER KEY

1. A, 2. C, 3. A, 4. C, 5. A, 6. B, 7. B, 8. T, 9. T, 10. T

CHAPTER 19

Archaeology and the Old Testament

You Should Know

- Archaeology: study of the material culture of the peoples of antiquity in hopes of reconstructing their history and lifestyles
- Ostraca: pieces of broken pottery that were sometimes written on
- Mari: city located on the upper Euphrates river that has an important archive
- Ebla: prominent third-millennium city with an important archive
- Amarna: archive that contains correspondence between Egyptian pharaohs and their vassals in the fourteenth century BC
- Ugarit: city-state and seaport in the Late Bronze Age with an archive that has shed light on biblical literature
- Dead Sea Scrolls: important cache of biblical scrolls found in the Dead Sea in 1948
- Archaeology is an important tool for reconstructing the lifestyle and history of ancient peoples, including those of the Bible.
- The primary contribution of archaeology to biblical studies is the illumination it provides about life in Bible times.
- There are important limitations concerning what archaeology can actually accomplish for the Bible.

Reflection Questions

1. What is the significance of archaeology for the Bible?

2. Describe what archaeology *cannot* do for the Bible and why.

Quiz

1. Excavations from Tel Dan have yielded inscriptions referring to the "house" of which king of Israel?

    a) David
    b) Manasseh
    c) Josiah
    d) Asa

2. The Stele of Shalmanseer III includes reference to which northern kings of Israel?

    a) Pekah and Baasha
    b) Jehoash and Jeroboam
    c) Ahab and Jehu
    d) Joram and Hoshea

3. The Dead Sea Scrolls were found in the _____.

    a) 1940s
    b) 1920s
    c) 1860s
    d) 1980s

4. The Sennacherib Prism records receiving tribute from which king of Judah?

    a) Uzziah
    b) Hezekiah
    c) Jehoshaphat
    d) David

5. Which of the following is not a site of a major archive?

    a) Mari
    b) Ebla
    c) Susa
    d) Nuzi

6. Which of the following is not a monument or inscription mentioned in the book that is important for biblical studies?
   a) Mesha Inscription
   b) Stele of Shalmaneser III
   c) Rosetta Stone
   d) Cyrus Cylinder

7. Which of the following is NOT a biblical person whom archeological findings have confirmed actually existed?
   a) Sennacherib
   b) Belshazzar
   c) Balaam
   d) Abraham

8. (T/F) The purpose of biblical archeology is to recover the material culture of the peoples of antiquity and, in so doing, attempt to reconstruct their history and lifestyles.

9. (T/F) Only a small amount of archaeological findings have been examined and published.

10. (T/F) The Mesha Inscription, though rich in information about ancient Hittite culture, is of little value to biblical studies because it makes no mention of Israel.

ANSWER KEY

1. A, 2. C, 3. A, 4. B, 5. C, 6. C, 7. D, 8. T, 9. T, 10. F

CHAPTER 20

Hebrew Poetic and Wisdom Literature

You Should Know

- Oracular prose: a hybrid literary form characteristic of OT prophetic books and combining elements of prose and poetry

- Superscription: a statement of classification and/or identification prefixed to a literary work

- Theodicy: the philosophical and/or theological defense of God's goodness and omnipotence in view of the existence of evil

- Acrostic: a poetic composition in which sets of sequential letters (e.g., initial or final letters of the lines) form a word or phrase or the alphabet

- Dirge: a funeral poem or song; a slow and mournful song or hymn of grief

- Alliteration: consonance of sounds at the beginning of words or syllables

- Assonance: the rhythm of sound using the correspondence of vowels, often at the ends of words

- Paronomasia: word play

- Onomatopoeia: use of words that sound like what they describe

- Ellipsis: omission of a word or words that would complete a parallel construction

- Inclusion: use of repeated words or phrases at the beginning and end of a piece of writing

Reflection Questions

1. What are the primary differences between biblical poetry and modern-day English poetry?

2. According to the Old Testament, what is wisdom? How does this differ from what is considered wisdom in the secular world?

Quiz

1. Poetry comprises _____ of the Old Testament.
   a) One-tenth
   b) One-quarter
   c) One-third
   d) One-half

2. The "Teachings of _____" from Egypt, bear a striking resemblance to portions of Proverbs 22:17–24:23.
   a) Gilgamesh
   b) Amenemope
   c) Hillel
   d) Marduk

3. The earliest Hebrew poetry extant dates to the _____ century BC.
   a) Ninth
   b) Fifth
   c) Thirteenth
   d) Seventh

4. All of the following are elements present in Hebrew poetry EXCEPT _____.
   a) Acrostic
   b) Alliteration
   c) Atonality
   d) Onomatopoeia

5. Which of the following is NOT a wisdom speech form?
   a) Parable

b) Song
   c) Riddle
   d) Fable

6. Which of the following is NOT an aspect of the fear of the Lord?
   a) Awe and reverence for God
   b) Dread at God's holiness
   c) Faith and trust in God's plan for human life
   d) Being intimate with the wicked

7. Which concept distinguished Hebrew wisdom from its ancient Near East counterparts?
   a) Fairness in judicial proceedings
   b) Punishment for wrongdoing
   c) Fair treatment of the weak
   d) The fear of the Lord

8. (T/F) Old Testament poetry is musical in nature and was usually intended to be sung.

9. (T/F) The notion of theodicy discussed in some wisdom literature deals primarily with God's instructions about marital faithfulness.

10. (T/F) True wisdom is a lifestyle.

ANSWER KEY

1. C, 2. B, 3. C, 4. C, 5. B, 6. D, 7. D, 8. T, 9. F, 10. T

CHAPTER 21

Job

You Should Know

- Theodicy: the philosophical and/or theological defense of God's goodness and omnipotence in view of the existence of evil

- Wisdom and poetic literature: Job, Psalms, Proverbs, Ecclesiastes, Song of Songs

- Retribution principle: the idea that there is a one-to-one correlation between one's actions and rewards

- "Man and His God": Sumerian literature that is a monologue that discusses suffering

- "The Babylonian Theodicy": Babylonian literature that is a dialogue between two people about suffering

- Mesopotamia: the land between the Tigris and Euphrates rivers

- The Book of Job confirms that God tends to act according to the retribution principle, but cautions that it cannot address the issue of causation.

- It is not true that only the wicked suffer.

- God's justice cannot be reduced to a simple formula like the retribution principle.

- God's infinite wisdom is the key to acknowledging his justice.

Reflection Questions

1. How would you resolve the problem of unjust suffering based on the Book of Job?

2. What is the Israelite view of the retribution principle? How does the book of Job confront it?

Quiz

1. The "place names" in the book of Job suggest that he may have been a(n) _____.

    a) Israelite
    b) Moabite
    c) Edomite
    d) Ammonite

2. Which of these men is NOT one of the three friends mentioned at the beginning of the book of Job?

    a) Eliphaz
    b) Elihu
    c) Bildad
    d) Zophar

3. Job's lament in chapter 3 introduces _____ cycles of dialogue which occupy chapters 4–27.

    a) Three
    b) Four
    c) Two
    d) Seven

4. Most simply stated, the retribution principle is that: If a person is righteous, he will _____ and if a person is wicked, he will _____.

    a) Tell the truth; lie
    b) Prosper; suffer
    c) Treat others well; treat others poorly
    d) Work; steal

5. Which of the following is NOT one of Job's three friends?

    a) Zophar
    b) Elihu

c) Bezalel
   d) Eliphaz

6. _____ is an ancient piece of literature similar to the book of Job.
   a) Gilgamesh Epic
   b) Babylonian Theodicy
   c) Mesha Stele
   d) The *Iliad*

7. Which of these is NOT a major theme in the book of Job?
   a) Retribution principle
   b) Mediator
   c) Wisdom, justice, and sovereignty
   d) Proper temple worship

8. (T/F) The Israelites view judgment as a civil case in which he is a plaintiff seeking justice.

9. (T/F) After Job is vindicated, God explains to Job that he had to suffer to bring God glory.

10. (T/F) Job does not feel that he needs a mediator.

ANSWER KEY

1. C, 2. B, 3. A, 4. B, 5. C, 6. B, 7. D, 8. T, 9. F, 10. F

CHAPTER 22

Psalms

You Should Know

- Wisdom and poetic literature: Job, Psalms, Proverbs, Ecclesiastes, Song of Songs
- Theocracy: a state or nation ruled directly by God
- Praise psalm: genre of psalm in which the focus is praise for the Lord
- Lament psalm: genre of psalm in which a complaint, or lament, is voiced
- Wisdom psalm: genre of psalm concerned with wise and righteous living
- Recognition of the kingship and sovereignty of God
- Conduct and destiny of the righteous and the wicked
- God's comfort and defense in times of crisis
- Importance of praise in all of its variations
- Role of nature and creation

Reflection Questions

1. Define the three major genres of psalms. Choose one and examine it in more detail.

2. How does the book of Psalms interact with the concepts of nature and creation? How does its portrayal of these themes apply today?

Quiz

1. The book of Psalms is divided into _____ "books."
   a) Three
   b) Four
   c) Five
   d) Seven

2. Which is not one of the major genres of psalms listed in the textbook?
   a) Enthronement
   b) Praise
   c) Lament
   d) Wisdom

3. What type of psalm is Psalm 1?
   a) Wisdom
   b) Praise
   c) Lament
   d) Enthronement

4. Book 1 contains mostly _____.
   a) Praises
   b) Laments
   c) Wisdom psalms
   d) Coronation psalms

5. All of the following people are an author of one or more psalms EXCEPT _____.
   a) Asaph
   b) The sons of Korah
   c) Moses
   d) Nathan

6. One of the major themes of the book of Psalms deals with kingship; there are _____ psalms scattered throughout the Psalter which concern the king.

a) 3
b) 7
c) 9
d) 18

7. The second part of the retribution principle can be summed up as: Those who _____ are righteous, while those who _____ are wicked.

   a) Prosper; suffer
   b) Pray; don't pray
   c) Worship God; don't worship God
   d) Keep God's commands; disobey God's commands

8. (T/F) Each category of psalm has typical characteristics and a fairly consistent format by which it can be identified.

9. (T/F) Some of our oldest manuscripts show varying arrangements of the books of Psalms before their present arrangement, as we know it in the Psalter today, was finalized.

10. (T/F) The Psalms' focus on nature and creation speaks directly against the Canaanite propensity to worship fertility gods/gods of nature.

ANSWER KEY

1. C, 2. A, 3. A, 4. B, 5. D, 6. C, 7. A, 8. T, 9. F, 10. T

CHAPTER 23

Proverbs

You Should Know

- Corpus: a collection of related writings
- Wisdom and poetic literature: Job, Psalms, Proverbs, Ecclesiastes, Song of Songs
- Retribution principle: the idea that there is a one-to-one correlation between one's actions and rewards
- Proverb: short, pithy statement that captures a basic truth
- Instructional literature: literature meant to provide instruction and guidance
- Sage: a wise person who taught others
- The fear of the Lord is the beginning of wisdom.
- The way of wisdom leads to life.
- A proverb illustrates a general principle, not a promise.
- Wisdom leads to an understanding of the retribution principle.

Reflection Questions

1. How does the book of Proverbs address the retribution principle compared to how it is addressed in Psalms?

2. What does Proverbs say about human speech? How would you apply this today?

Quiz

1. Which of the following is NOT a major theme of the book of Proverbs?

    a) Human sexuality
    b) The fear of the Lord
    c) Possessing the land
    d) Human speech

2. The book of Proverbs contains _____ collections of wise sayings.

    a) Three
    b) Five
    c) Eight
    d) Eleven

3. The biblical wisdom literature acknowledges which god?

    a) Yahweh
    b) Thoth
    c) Aten
    d) Shamash

4. All of the following were contributors to the book of Proverbs EXCEPT _____.

    a) Agur
    b) Lemuel of Massa
    c) Amenemope
    d) Solomon

5. Proverbs 31:10–31 is an acrostic poem extolling the virtues of the ideal _____.

    a) Son
    b) Brother
    c) Wife
    d) King

6. Which of the following is NOT a wisdom speech form that Proverbs uses?

a) Numerical sayings
b) Wisdom discourse
c) Call and response
d) Acrostic poem

7. Which of the following is NOT one of the three institutions where instruction centered?

a) Family
b) Royal court
c) Marketplace
d) Scribal schools

8. (T/F) The book of Proverbs encourages its hearers to embrace integrity, justice, righteousness, and life.

9. (T/F) Proverbs asserts that there is great power in human speech, both for good and evil.

10. (T/F) The message of Proverbs hinges on the belief that wisdom cannot be taught but must be intuited naturally.

ANSWER KEY

1. C, 2. C, 3. A, 4. C, 5. C, 6. C, 7. C, 8. T, 9. T, 10. F

CHAPTER 24

Ecclesiastes

You Should Know

- Wisdom and poetic literature: Job, Psalms, Proverbs, Ecclesiastes, Song of Songs

- Retribution principle: the idea that there is a one-to-one correlation between one's actions and rewards

- Epicureanism: philosophical viewpoint that people should "eat, drink, and be merry, for tomorrow we die"

- Instructional literature: literature meant to provide instruction and guidance

- Sage: a wise person who taught others

- Qoheleth: the speaker in the book of Ecclesiastes

- Life should not be expected to be self-fulfilling.

- Frustrations in life are inevitable.

- The seasons of life must be accepted.

- Enjoyment of life comes only through a God-centered worldview.

Reflection Questions

1. Should Christians enjoy life? Explain.

2. What is the meaning of the phrase "under the sun" in Ecclesiastes? How does the author use it to accomplish his purpose of writing?

Quiz

1. All of the following are key ideas from the book of Ecclesiastes EXCEPT _____.

    a) Frustrations in life are unavoidable
    b) The seasons of life must be accepted
    c) Life should not be expected to be self-fulfilling
    d) Enjoyment in life comes through our arranging for it

2. The wisdom of Ecclesiastes comes from the "Qoheleth" which means _____.

    a) Judge
    b) Sage/wise man
    c) Teacher/preacher
    d) Servant

3. The school of the rabbi _____, like many through history, questioned the authority of Ecclesiastes and its canonical status.

    a) Hillel
    b) Shammai
    c) Akiva
    d) Judah ben Tabbai

4. Literarily Ecclesiastes makes use of all of the following EXCEPT for _____.

    a) Allegories
    b) Metaphors
    c) Proverbs
    d) Sonnets

5. The Qoheleth repeatedly uses the phrase _____ to speak of life and experience in the world.

    a) "On the earth"
    b) "In the land"
    c) "Under the sun"
    d) "Beneath the heavens"

6. According to Qoheleth, life is _____.

   a) A gift from God
   b) A great burden
   c) Not worth living
   d) Something humans do not deserve

7. What is the solution that Qoheleth offers regarding adversity?

   a) We should always overcome it
   b) We should run from it
   c) We should not try to avoid it
   d) We deserve it

8. (T/F) The book of Ecclesiastes is wholly pessimistic.

9. (T/F) Qoheleth contends that nothing under the sun can give meaning to life.

10. (T/F) The Qoheleth promotes an "eat, drink, and be merry for tomorrow we die" view of the world.

ANSWER KEY

1. D, 2. C, 3. B, 4. D, 5. C, 6. A, 7. C, 8. F, 9. T, 10. F

CHAPTER 25

Song of Songs

You Should Know

- Provenance: the original source, setting, or locale for a literary work.

- Megilloth: the Hebrew word for "scrolls" or "rolls." The term is used to describe the five books in the Hebrew Bible read publicly during the annual festivals of the Jewish religious calendar (Song of Songs – Passover; Ruth – Pentecost; Lamentations – Fast of Ab, the commemoration of the destruction of the temple; Ecclesiastes – Tabernacles; Esther – Purim)

- Wisdom and poetic literature: Job, Psalms, Proverbs, Ecclesiastes, Song of Songs

- Solomon: third king of Israel traditionally considered to be the author of Song of Songs

- Typology: one aspect of biblical interpretation that establishes a correspondence between OT events, person, objects, and/or ideas ("type") and their NT counterparts ("antetype") by way of foreshadowing or prototype

- Allegory: obvious symbolic representation in literature (extended metaphor)

- The goodness of humanity created male and female in God's image

- The dignity of human affections

- The sanctity of human sexual expression in the context of marriage

- The virtue of chastity before marriage and the virtue of faithfulness once married

Reflection Questions

1. Describe three of the seven methods for interpreting Song of Songs.

2. How does Song of Songs apply to the Christian life today?

Quiz

1. In the Hebrew Scripture Song of Songs is in the _____.
    a) Torah
    b) Latter Prophets
    c) Writings
    d) The Twelve

2. Authorship of Songs of Songs is traditionally attributed to _____.
    a) David
    b) Nathan
    c) Jeremiah
    d) Solomon

3. In later Judaism Song of Songs was designated to be read as a part of which feast, since it was understood to represent God's love for Israel?
    a) Passover
    b) Purim
    c) Yom Kippur
    d) Sukkot (Feast of Tabernacles)

4. Which of these represents an interpretative approach that has been taken with Song of Songs?
    a) Wedding Cycle
    b) Allegorical
    c) Literal
    d) All of the above

5. Which of the following people is NOT featured in Song of Songs?

a) Solomon
b) A Shulammite maiden
c) A village priest
d) A shepherd lover

6. Which of the following is the oldest interpretive approach to Song of Songs?

    a) Allegorical
    b) Cultic
    c) Didactic
    d) Literal

7. Which of the following is not a characteristic of lyric love poetry found in Song of Songs?

    a) Emphasis on emotion
    b) Abrupt shifts in scene
    c) Inappropriate language
    d) Unifying theme

8. (T/F) Song of Songs can be considered lyric love poetry.

9. (T/F) Song of Songs affirms chastity for unmarried people.

10. (T/F) There are multiple clear historical allusions in Song of Songs.

ANSWER KEY

1. C, 2. D, 3. A, 4. D, 5. C, 6. A, 7. C, 8. T, 9. T, 10. F

CHAPTER 26

Formation of the Old Testament Scriptures

You Should Know

- Masoretes: Jewish scholars and scribes who preserved the Hebrew Bible, improved word divisions, and added vowels, punctuation marks, and verse divisions (roughly between AD 500 and 900)

- Textual criticism: the science of comparing the variant readings of biblical manuscripts for the purpose of establishing the contents of the original text

- Messenger formula: the clause "[koh] 'amar YHWH ..." ("so Yahweh [has] said"), introducing a messenger speech (or prophetic oracle) and signifying the oral transmission of a message by means of a third party

- Pseudepigrapha: extra-canonical Jewish literature of the intertestamental period

- Greek Septuagint: Greek translation of the Old Testament

- Canon: the list or collection of books comprising the Hebrew Scriptures

- The Old Testament was composed over a thousand-year period from the mid-second to mid-first millennium BC.

- The earliest manuscripts of the OT were composed in Hebrew.

- Textual criticism is necessary because of human error introduced into copies of the biblical text.

- The OT canon was fixed by the time of Christ.

Reflection Questions

1. Is the Bible we have today reliable? Explain.

2. What are the selection criteria for the canon of the Old Testament? Why does this matter for Christians today?

Quiz

1. At least _____ different writers have been identified as human authors of the Old Testament.
   a) Twenty
   b) Thirty
   c) Forty
   d) Fifty

2. What was the earliest stage in the development of writing?
   a) Syllables
   b) Pictograms
   c) Logograms
   d) Alphabetic script

3. Which important group of Jewish scholars improved word divisions, and added vowel points, punctuation marks, and verse divisions to the Hebrew Old Testament?
   a) The Qumranites
   b) The Masoretes
   c) The Levites
   d) The sons of Korah

4. What are human errors of sight, hearing, writing, memory, and judgment which occur during the hand-copying process known as?
   a) Typos
   b) Variants
   c) Oops
   d) Blunders

5. Which of the following attested to the tri-partite division of the Old Testament?

a) Jesus
b) Jeremiah
c) Moses
d) Abraham

6. Who held that the Apocrypha, though not Scripture, was useful for edification?

a) Jerome
b) Irenaeus
c) Luther
d) Calvin

7. Who is responsible for removing the Apocrypha from the English Bible?

a) Puritans
b) King Henry VIII
c) Queen Elizabeth I
d) Anabaptists

8. (T/F) The religious leaders of the Hebrew community established the canon.

9. (T/F) The word *Apocrypha* means "hidden" and refers to a group of books produced during the time of the exile in Babylon.

10. (T/F) The Hebrews included twenty-four books in the Holy Scriptures, which is fifteen less than the English Old Testament, but they both contain the exact same material.

ANSWER KEY

1. C, 2. B, 3. B, 4. B, 5. A, 6. C, 7. A, 8. T, 9. F, 10. T

CHAPTER 27

Introduction to Prophetic Literature

You Should Know

- Eschatology: that branch of theology concerned with end-time events (i.e., the doctrine of the last things)

- *Nabî*: OT title for a prophet that indicates the prophet is "one who is called"

- Baal: the Canaanite storm god, deity of agriculture and reproductive fertility

- Preclassical prophecy: prophecy before the eighth century BC; we have no books written by preclassical prophets, who ministered primarily to the monarchy

- Classical prophecy: prophecy that began in the eighth century BC; we have many writings from these prophets who ministered to both kings and people

- The prophetic office existed across the ancient Near East.

- Prophecy in Israel is divided into preclassical and classical prophecy.

- Classical prophecy has no ancient Near Eastern counterpart.

- The role of the prophet was to communicate God's message.

- Prediction and fulfillment must be understood correctly to avoid misperceptions about the nature of prophecy.

Reflection Questions

1. What is the difference between classical prophecy and pre-classical prophecy?

2. How should apocalyptic literature be interpreted and applied today?

Quiz

1. The ministry of biblical prophets tended to be clustered around _____.

    a) The eighth century BC
    b) Times of peace
    c) The city of Samaria
    d) Times of crisis

2. The best example of a pre-classical prophet who held the reins of leadership was _____.

    a) Elijah
    b) Amos
    c) Moses
    d) Joel

3. _____ can be characterized as apocalyptic literature.

    a) Daniel and Zechariah
    b) Hosea and Amos
    c) Isaiah and Jeremiah
    d) Obadiah and Nahum

4. In general, the progression of the role of the prophet within Israel was _____.

    a) Leader, adviser, and social/spiritual commentator
    b) Adviser, social/spiritual commentator, and leader
    c) Social/spiritual commentator, leader, and adviser
    d) Leader, social/spiritual commentator, and adviser

5. The earliest of the classical prophets who were active within Israel (the northern kingdom) were _____.

a) Obadiah and Habakkuk
b) Amos and Hosea
c) Isaiah and Micah
d) Jonah and Zephaniah

6. All of the following are tips for reading prophetic literature EXCEPT _____.

    a) Think of prophecy as God's syllabus
    b) Identify the category to which an oracle belongs
    c) Determine what current event the prophecy is tied to
    d) Distinguish between the message of the prophecy and the fulfillment of the prophecy

7. All of the following are types of oracles present within prophetic literature EXCEPT _____.

    a) Indictment oracles
    b) Judgment oracles
    c) Instruction oracles
    d) Grief oracles

8. (T/F) A prophet is someone who speaks on behalf of someone else.

9. (T/F) The prophet's job was to communicate a message from God.

10. (T/F) The primary job of a prophet is to highlight what the people are doing correctly.

ANSWER KEY

1. D, 2. C, 3. A, 4. A, 5. B, 6. C, 7. D, 8. T, 9. T, 10. F

CHAPTER 28

Isaiah

You Should Know

- Isaiah: eighth-century prophet to Judah
- Cyrus: Medo-Persian king who defeated the Babylonian Empire
- Assyrian Empire: major power in the ancient Near East ca. 1076–612 BC
- Tiglath-Pileser III: Neo-Assyrian king who invaded Israel
- Sennacherib: Assyrian king who invaded Judah in 701 BC
- Babylonian Empire: major power in the ancient Near East ca. 612–539 BC
- The trustworthiness of the Lord
- The incomparability of Israel's God
- Divine sovereignty in judgment and deliverance
- God's address to those who would return from exile

Reflection Questions

1. Choose one of the major themes of Isaiah and discuss its significance for the Christian life.

2. Describe the historical background of the book of Isaiah.

Quiz

1. The prophet Isaiah lived in the _____ century BC.

a) Fourth
b) Sixth
c) Seventh
d) Eighth

2. One of the biggest controversies surrounding the book of Isaiah is in relation to its _____.

a) Syntax
b) Vocabulary
c) Unity
d) Themes

3. How many major sections/scenarios is the book of Isaiah divided into?

a) Two
b) Four
c) Five
d) Six

4. Which two kings of Judah feature prominently in the book of Isaiah?

a) Ahaz and Hezekiah
b) Jotham and Manasseh
c) Josiah and Jehoiakim
d) Uzziah and Amaziah

5. All of the following are major themes in the book of Isaiah EXCEPT _____.

a) Redeemer
b) The Servant
c) Hesed
d) The Holy One of Israel

6. Which Assyrian king invaded Israel in the eighth century?

a) Tiglath-Pileser III
b) Tiglath-Pileser II
c) Narum-Sin
d) Cyrus

7. Which Babylonian king invaded Judah in the eighth century?
   a) Tiglath-Pileser III
   b) Narum-Sin
   c) Sennacherib
   d) Cyrus

8. (T/F) The background of Isaiah is the invasion of Israel by the Neo-Babylonian Empire.

9. (T/F) The material of the book is arranged to highlight the trustworthiness of the covenant God.

10. (T/F) The New Testament attributes parts of the second half of the book of Isaiah to the prophet Isaiah.

ANSWER KEY

1. D, 2. C, 3. B, 4. A, 5. C, 6. A, 7. C, 8. F, 9. T, 10. T

CHAPTER 29

Jeremiah

You Should Know

- Jeremiah: seventh-century prophet of Judah
- Babylonian Empire: major power in the ancient Near East ca. 612–539 BC
- Covenant: the means by which God reveals himself to, initiates relationship with, and establishes his presence among humanity by entering into a mutually binding agreement with a person or people
- Vassal: a subordinate nation or people group (usually as a result of a treaty following conquest)
- Oracle: an authoritative prophetic speech
- "Confessions" of Jeremiah: series of laments and complaints from Jeremiah to the Lord
- The law in the heart
- God's policy for dealing with the nations
- God's bringing an enemy against Israel
- God as the potter who destroys and builds up

Reflection Questions

1. Why would the book of Jeremiah include Jeremiah's complaints? Explain.

2. What is "new" about the new covenant?

Quiz

1. Jeremiah functioned as a prophet during which crisis in Israel's history?

    a) The Assyrian invasion
    b) The fall of Jerusalem
    c) The great locust plague
    d) The split of the northern and southern kingdoms

2. Jeremiah's scribe was _____.

    a) Baruch
    b) Ezra
    c) Eliezer
    d) Accroupi

3. Jeremiah contains _____ major books/sections.

    a) 2
    b) 3
    c) 5
    d) 7

4. Who was king when Jeremiah began his ministry?

    a) Ahab
    b) David
    c) Hezekiah
    d) Josiah

5. The nation of Judah was conquered by _____.

    a) Babylon
    b) Assyria
    c) Egypt
    d) Rome

6. The fall of Jerusalem occurred in _____.

    a) 722 BC
    b) 587/6 BC
    c) AD 30
    d) AD 70

7. All of the following are major themes in the book of Jeremiah EXCEPT _____.
   a) The New Covenant
   b) God's policy with the nations
   c) False prophets
   d) The new temple

8. (T/F) Jeremiah deals with the issue of God's judgment of nations due to generations of compounded sin.

9. (T/F) Though Jeremiah is called to deliver a difficult message he seems to have been able to carry out his duty as a prophet without any substantial personal struggles.

10. (T/F) By Jeremiah's time all of the false prophets had been expelled from Judah.

ANSWER KEY

1. B, 2. A, 3. B, 4. D, 5. A, 6. B, 7. D, 8. T, 9. F, 10. F

CHAPTER 30

Lamentations

You Should Know

- Lamentation: expression of grief over a catastrophe that is irreversible
- Catharsis: purification, especially a purging of the emotions that brings release from anxiety and guilt and yields spiritual renewal
- Dirge: a funeral poem or song; a slow and mournful song or hymn of grief
- Acrostic: a poetic composition in which sets of sequential letters (e.g., initial or final letters of the lines) form a word or phrase or an alphabet
- Covenant: the means by which God reveals himself to, initiates relationship with, and establishes his presence among humanity by entering into a mutually binding agreement with a person or people
- Zion: a poetic name for the city of Israel
- God punishes sin.
- God's judgment is just.
- God instructs the faithful through suffering.
- God is faithful, instilling hope in the righteous.

Reflection Questions

1. Did God abandon his people during the exile? Explain.

2. What are the various types of suffering experienced by humans? How can a person know which type she is experiencing?

Quiz

1. Both the Septuagint and Jewish tradition ascribe authorship of Lamentations to _____.
   a) Jeremiah
   b) Isaiah
   c) Habakkuk
   d) Solomon

2. The book of Lamentations mourns the fall of Jerusalem in _____.
   a) 722/721 BC
   b) 682/681 BC
   c) 587/586 BC
   d) 528/527 BC

3. The book of Lamentations is concerned with the defeat and exile of _____.
   a) Israel
   b) Judah
   c) Egypt
   d) Babylon

4. The book of Lamentations is comprised of five poems, three of which are _____, opening with the customary wail "how?"
   a) Prayers
   b) Funeral dirges
   c) Acrostics
   d) Imprecatory appeals

5. Who was the king of Babylon when Jerusalem fell?
   a) Nabopolassar
   b) Nabonidus
   c) Nebuchadrezzar
   d) Darius

6. Most of the poems of Lamentations are composed as _____.

a) Acrostics
b) Linear thoughts
c) Cycles
d) Narratives

7. (T/F) Lamentations illustrates the retributive aspect of human suffering; at least some suffering is brought on as punishment.

8. (T/F) Two of the poems of Lamentations are cast in the form of a "lament" or "complaint."

9. (T/F) The book of Lamentations teaches that God does not punish sin.

10. (T/F) The book of Lamentations teaches that God will not forever abandon his people.

ANSWER KEY
1. A, 2. C, 3. B, 4. B, 5. C, 6. A, 7. T, 8. T, 9. F, 10. T

CHAPTER 31

Ezekiel

You Should Know

- Ezekiel: seventh-century prophet of Judah
- Great Synagogue: a council of scribes and other Hebrew leaders reputedly founded after the Babylonian exile to reorganize Jewish religious life and culture
- Proto-apocalyptic: an OT prototype of apocalyptic literature that contains some of the elements and features of later intertestamental apocalyptic literature
- Babylonian Empire: major power in the ancient Near East ca. 612–539 BC
- Yahweh's sovereignty over Israel and the nations
- Dynamic relationship of the individual to the group
- Mysterious interplay of individual responsibility and divine judgment
- Babylonian exile as punishment for Judah's sin of idolatry
- Yahweh's faithfulness to his covenant promises
- Restoration of a New Israel under Davidic leadership

Reflection Questions

1. In what ways is it significant that Ezekiel ministered outside of Judah's national boundaries?

2. Explain the purpose of Ezekiel's chariot vision and its application to the Christian life today.

Quiz

1. Ezekiel was a _____.

    a) Magistrate
    b) Priest
    c) Scribe
    d) Farmer

2. The canonical value of Ezekiel was called into question because of _____.

    a) The prophet's understanding of temple ritual
    b) The lack of the use of the name of God in the book
    c) Several sections containing erotic poetry portraying human love
    d) Ezekiel's questioning of the Davidic line of kings

3. How many times does Ezekiel's chariot vision appear in the text?

    a) One
    b) Two
    c) Three
    d) Four

4. Ezekiel prophesied during the captivity by which nation?

    a) Assyria
    b) Egypt
    c) Babylon
    d) Persia

5. Which of the following features is NOT indicative of apocalyptic literature?

    a) Strange visions and unusual symbols
    b) Eschatological judgment
    c) Divine absence in human history
    d) The ultimate victory of God

6. Ezekiel has been known as the _____.

    a) Watchman
    b) Watchdog

c) Lookout
d) Spy

7. The Lord addresses Ezekiel by the title "_____" some ninety times in the book.

   a) Prophet
   b) Son of Man
   c) Mighty Man
   d) Son of Buzi

8. (T/F) Several elements of apocalyptic literature reside in the writings of Ezekiel.

9. (T/F) The purpose of the book of Ezekiel was to promote the rebuilding of the temple.

10. (T/F) The book of Ezekiel is essentially a theodicy.

ANSWER KEY

1. B, 2. A, 3. C, 4. C, 5. C, 6. A, 7. B, 8. T, 9. F, 10. T

Chapter 32

Daniel

You Should Know

- Pseudonymity: the literary device of writing under a false or assumed name; commonly recognized as a feature of apocalyptic literature

- Babylonian Empire: major power in the ancient Near East ca. 612–539 BC

- Persian Empire: major power in the ancient Near East ca. 539–332 BC

- Cyrus: Medo-Persian king who defeated the Babylonian Empire

- *Vaticinium ex eventu*: lit. "prophecy from the event," this term refers to "prophecies" that purport to be prophetic but were in fact written after the event occurred

- Eschatology: the branch of theology concerned with end-time events (i.e., the doctrine of last things)

- Living a life of faith in an increasingly hostile world

- Sovereignty of God to deliver and prosper people of faith

- Sovereignty of God in international political affairs

- The downfall of the earthly kings is their pride, while the downfall of Israel was her rebellion against God.

Reflection Questions

1. Explain the concept of *vaticuinium ex eventu* and its importance for the book of Daniel.

2. Choose one of the two major themes for the book of Daniel and explain their significance for and application to the Christian life today.

Quiz

1. Daniel was trained in diplomatic service and served in the _____ government.
    a) Assyrian
    b) Egyptian
    c) Hittite
    d) Babylonian

2. The book of Daniel is written in Hebrew and has a large section written in _____.
    a) Akkadian
    b) Aramaic
    c) Ugaritic
    d) Syriac

3. How many kingdoms are featured in the visions of Daniel chapters 2 and 7?
    a) Three
    b) Four
    c) Six
    d) Seven

4. Who was welcomed into Babylon as a deliverer?
    a) Xerxes
    b) Artaxerxes
    c) Cyrus
    d) Darius

5. The book of Daniel divides clearly between chapters _____ and _____.
    a) 6, 7
    b) 7, 8

c) 2, 3
   d) 4, 5

6. Some scholars attribute the writing of the book of Daniel to an author in the second century BC due to very precise predictions in chapter 11 relating to which world empire?

   a) Persian
   b) Roman
   c) Greek
   d) Egyptian

7. Which kingdom is under discussion in chapter 11?

   a) Greek
   b) Roman
   c) Babylonian
   d) Medo-Persian

8. (T/F) The sovereignty of God is one of the core messages of Daniel.

9. (T/F) Though Daniel and his friends reside in a pagan nation, the surrounding culture appears to be amiable toward Israelite religion.

10. (T/F) The four kingdoms in chapters 2 and 7 are clearly identified.

ANSWER KEY

1. D, 2. B, 3. B, 4. C, 5. A, 6. C, 7. A, 8. T, 9. F, 10. F

CHAPTER 33

Hosea

You Should Know

- Palistrophe: a chiastic literary device that inverts or counterbalances key themes hinging upon one fundamental teaching or idea
- Minor Prophets: known as "The Twelve" in the Hebrew Bible, they are Hosea, Amos, Jonah, Micah, Nahum, Habakkuk, Zephaniah, Obadiah, Joel, Haggai, Zechariah, and Malachi
- Neo-Assyrian period: middle and late 700s BC, the time during which Hosea prophesied
- Hosea: eighth-century prophet to Israel
- 722 BC: year that Samaria fell
- Covenant: the means by which God reveals himself to, initiates relationship with, and establishes his presence among humanity by entering into a mutually binding agreement with a person or people; illustrates Yahweh's unchanging love for Israel
- Yahweh's jealousy for his covenant
- Yahweh's just judgment
- Yahweh's healing and restoration of the remnant

Reflection Questions

1. Why is marriage such a powerful metaphor for Yahweh's relationship with Israel?

2. Describe the various interpretive options for Hosea's marriage to Gomer.

Quiz

1. Hosea the prophet operated during the northern kingdom's "golden age" under King _____.

    a) Jehu
    b) Jeroboam II
    c) Omri
    d) Pekah

2. God commanded Hosea to marry a _____ named Gomer.

    a) Prostitute
    b) Handmaiden
    c) Servant girl
    d) Baroness

3. The Canaanite god Baal was a god of _____.

    a) The sea
    b) The sun
    c) Warfare
    d) Fertility

4. Chapters 1–3 of Hosea are arranged in a literary pattern known as _____.

    a) Palistrophe
    b) Acrostic
    c) Dirge
    d) Epigram

5. Hosea was a prophet to which kingdom?

    a) Judah
    b) Israel
    c) Egypt
    d) Assyria

6. Hosea is part of the _____.

    a) Minor Prophets
    b) Major Prophets

c) Pentateuch
d) Wisdom Literature

7. Which of the following nations was NOT exerting pressure on Israel during Hosea's ministry?

    a) Egypt
    b) Assyria
    c) Babylon
    d) Judah

8. Which of the following is NOT an interpretive option for Hosea's marriage to Gomer?

    a) Symbolic marriage
    b) One literal marriage: sequential narrative
    c) Two literal marriages
    d) Three literal marriages

9. (T/F) One of the purposes of the book of Hosea was to highlight the spiritual harlotry of Israel.

10. (T/F) Legal terminology abounds in Hosea as God brings a "lawsuit" against Israel.

ANSWER KEY

1. B, 2. A, 3. D, 4. A, 5. B, 6. A, 7. C, 8. D, 9. T, 10. T

CHAPTER 34

Joel

You Should Know

- Minor Prophets: known as "The Twelve" in the Hebrew Bible, they are Hosea, Amos, Jonah, Micah, Nahum, Habakkuk, Zephaniah, Obadiah, Joel, Haggai, Zechariah, and Malachi
- Postexilic: period after the expulsion of Israel and Judah from the land
- Preexilic: period before the expulsion of Israel and Judah from the land
- Covenant: the means by which God reveals himself to, initiates relationship with, and establishes his presence among humanity by entering into a mutually binding agreement with a person or people
- "The day of the LORD": eschatological day of judgment
- Eschatology: that branch of theology concerned with end-time events (i.e., the doctrine of the last things)
- Joel is primarily concerned to address "the day of the LORD."
- Calls on the people to repent, and when the people respond positively, he announces a coming period of prosperity
- Analogy of the locust plague to describe the coming day of the LORD
- The pouring out of the Spirit on all people as a prelude to judgment

Reflection Questions

1. Is Peter correct in applying Joel 2:28–32 to the Day of Pentecost? Explain.

2. What is the Day of the LORD? What is its relevance to the Christian life today?

Quiz

1. The book of Joel abundantly uses words, phrases, and motifs from which prophetic books?

   a) Malachi, Habakkuk, and Zechariah
   b) Isaiah, Amos, and Ezekiel
   c) Amos, Malachi, and Obadiah
   d) Isaiah, Habakkuk, and Zephaniah

2. Joel uses the image of _____ to speak of impending invasion and devastation.

   a) Malnourished cows
   b) Withering crops
   c) A locust plague
   d) An epidemic of bubonic plague

3. One of the difficult interpretive issues for Joel is its _____.

   a) Date
   b) Type of writing
   c) Authorship
   d) Content

4. Joel is part of the _____.

   a) Minor Prophets
   b) Major Prophets
   c) Pentateuch
   d) Wisdom Literature

5. The book of Joel is quoted in:

   a) 1 Peter
   b) 2 Peter
   c) Acts
   d) Galatians

6. What is the strongest evidence for Joel as a postexilic prophet?
   a) The use of the prophetic perfect
   b) Reference to the exile as a past event
   c) Reference to Babylon
   d) The mention of Baal worship

7. Prior to becoming a prophet Joel was a _____.
   a) Farmer
   b) Merchant
   c) Priest
   d) None of the above

8. (T/F) Joel prophetically identified a current crisis as God's judgment on the community.

9. (T/F) The book of Joel is quoted by Peter in his message on the day of Pentecost.

10. (T/F) One of Joel's major indictments of Israel is in relation to the worship of Baal.

ANSWER KEY

1. B, 2. C, 3. A, 4. A, 5. C, 6. B, 7. D, 8. T, 9. T, 10. F

CHAPTER 35

Amos

You Should Know

- Minor Prophets: known as "The Twelve" in the Hebrew Bible, they are Hosea, Amos, Jonah, Micah, Nahum, Habakkuk, Zephaniah, Obadiah, Joel, Haggai, Zechariah, and Malachi
- Preexilic: period before the expulsion of Israel and Judah from the land
- Covenant: the means by which God reveals himself to, initiates relationship with, and establishes his presence among humanity by entering into a mutually binding agreement with a person or people
- Amos: eighth-century prophet to Israel
- Neo-Assyrian Empire: major power in the ancient Near East ca. 911–612 BC
- Jeroboam II: wicked king of Israel who ruled during the ministry of Amos
- God holds the nations accountable for their social policy.
- Israel will not escape the judgment of the day of the Lord.
- True worship spawns social justice.
- God will restore a remnant of Israel.

Reflection Questions

1. What is the relationship between social justice and the gospel?
2. What does the epilogue of Amos indicate about Yahweh's covenant with Israel?

Quiz

1. Prior to becoming a prophet Amos was a _____.

    a) Priest
    b) Magistrate
    c) Shepherd
    d) Soldier

2. Amos's prophecies were delivered to Israel at _____, a site of syncretic worship.

    a) Samaria
    b) Bethel
    c) Dan
    d) Hazor

3. What natural phenomenon/event is referenced in Amos 1:1?

    a) An earthquake
    b) A whirlwind
    c) A famine
    d) A tidal wave

4. A major theme in the book of Amos is _____.

    a) Temple worship
    b) Intermarriage with surrounding pagan peoples
    c) The day of the LORD
    d) Social justice

5. Amos dated his prophecy by reference to which two kings?

    a) Uzziah and Jeroboam II
    b) Hezekiah and Hoshea
    c) Jehoash and Amaziah
    d) Pekah and Jotham

6. By what type of natural disaster does Amos date his ministry?

    a) Tornado
    b) Thunderstorm
    c) Earthquake
    d) Volcano eruption

7. Amos is from which city?
   a) Jerusalem
   b) Tekoa
   c) Samaria
   d) Bethelehem

8. Which NT book also deals with social justice?
   a) Matthew
   b) Galatians
   c) Romans
   d) James

9. (T/F) Amos says mistreatment of the poor is a symptom of spiritual sickness.

10. (T/F) Amos preached during a prosperous period in Israel's history.

ANSWER KEY

1. C, 2. B, 3. A, 4. D, 5. A, 6. C, 7. B, 8. D, 9. T, 10. T

CHAPTER 36

Obadiah

You Should Know

- Signet: a stamp or symbol of authority imprinted by means of a seal (as on a ring)
- Minor Prophets: known as "The Twelve" in the Hebrew Bible, they are Hosea, Amos, Jonah, Micah, Nahum, Habakkuk, Zephaniah, Obadiah, Joel, Haggai, Zechariah, and Malachi
- Edom: neighboring enemy nation of Israel
- Obadiah: prophet who prophesied against Edom
- Neo-Assyrian Empire: major power in the ancient Near East ca. 911–612 BC
- The prophet also addresses the godly remnant of Israel.
- Promised deliverance and restoration of the people at the consummation of God's kingdom
- The sovereignty of God over the nations
- The principle of retribution
- The restoration of Israel

Reflection Questions

1. Would Obadiah's message against Edom be considered "Christian" if delivered today? Explain.

2. What does Obadiah's concern with the restoration of Israel indicate about Yahweh's covenant relationship with his people? Explain.

Quiz

1. The book of Obadiah pronounces divine judgment on what nation?
   a) Babylon
   b) Edom
   c) Assyria
   d) Damascus

2. Obadiah is the _____ book in the Old Testament.
   a) Oldest
   b) Shortest
   c) Longest
   d) Last

3. The most likely background for the book of Obadiah is _____.
   a) The fall of Samaria
   b) The death of King Hezekiah
   c) The fall of Jerusalem
   d) The Edict of Cyrus

4. The book of Obadiah espouses the idea of *Lex Talionis* which means _____.
   a) "To the victor go the spoils"
   b) "An eye for an eye"
   c) "Seize the day"
   d) "Never give up"

5. Which of the following is NOT another name for Edom in the book of Obadiah?
   a) Hor
   b) Seir
   c) Jacob
   d) Esau

6. Obadiah's oracle is a _____.
   a) Dream
   b) Trance

c) Vision
d) Spoken-word event

7. Which of the following books does not contain an anti-Edomite oracle?

   a) Ezekiel
   b) Amos
   c) Isaiah
   d) Malachi

8. (T/F) One of the major reasons for which Obadiah proclaims judgment on this pagan nation is because of its pride.

9. (T/F) Obadiah's name means "the LORD will triumph."

10. (T/F) Obadiah is concerned with social justice and the spiritual sickness which is at the root of people's mistreatment of the poor.

ANSWER KEY

1. B, 2. B, 3. C, 4. B, 5. C, 6. C, 7. D, 8. T, 9. F, 10. F

CHAPTER 37

Jonah

You Should Know

- Minor Prophets: known as "The Twelve" in the Hebrew Bible, they are Hosea, Amos, Jonah, Micah, Nahum, Habakkuk, Zephaniah, Obadiah, Joel, Haggai, Zechariah, and Malachi
- Neo-Assyrian period: middle and late 700s BC, the time during which Jonah prophesied
- Neo-Assyrian Empire: major power in the ancient Near East ca. 911–612 BC
- Jonah: eighth-century Israelite prophet
- 722 BC: year that Samaria fell to Assyria
- Covenant: the means by which God reveals himself to, initiates relationship with, and establishes his presence among humanity by entering into a mutually binding agreement with a person or people
- Nineveh: major Assyrian city in which Jonah ministered
- God's right to perform gracious acts of compassion
- God's delight in small steps in the right direction
- God's propensity for offering second chances

Reflection Questions

1. How does Jonah engage the doctrines of divine sovereignty and human responsibility?

2. How is Jonah's interaction with theodicy different from that of Job and Ecclesiastes?

Quiz

1. The book of Jonah concerns the judgment of the city of Nineveh, the capital of _____.

    a) Babylon
    b) Damascus
    c) Assyria
    d) Persia

2. When Jonah sees that God has relented from destroying Nineveh because of their repentance he is _____.

    a) Excited
    b) Confused
    c) Relieved
    d) Angry

3. The book of Jonah is structured with _____ roughly even sections.

    a) Two
    b) Three
    c) Four
    d) Five

4. At the end of the book of Jonah, God is _____ toward the Ninevites.

    a) Compassionate
    b) Angry
    c) Unforgiving
    d) Frustrated

5. Jonah's theodicy is concerned with _____.

    a) Unjust suffering
    b) Death of the righteous
    c) Leniency toward wickedness
    d) God's anger

6. Jonah is angry because the people of Nineveh _____.

a) Mock him
b) Repent
c) Refuse to repent
d) Worship other gods

7. The book of Jonah is primarily concerned with _____.

a) Jonah
b) Nineveh
c) Cattle
d) God

8. (T/F) In interpreting the book, Jonah should be equated with the city of Nineveh.

9. (T/F) In the book of Jonah, Jonah represents Israel as a whole.

10. (T/F) The message of the book of Jonah is directed toward Israel, encouraging her to move beyond her borders to evangelize other nations and to love and forgive her enemies.

ANSWER KEY

1. C, 2. D, 3. A, 4. A, 5. C, 6. B, 7. D, 8. T, 9. F, 10. F

CHAPTER 38

Micah

You Should Know

- Minor Prophets: known as "The Twelve" in the Hebrew Bible, they are Hosea, Amos, Jonah, Micah, Nahum, Habakkuk, Zephaniah, Obadiah, Joel, Haggai, Zechariah, and Malachi

- Neo-Assyrian period: middle and late 700s BC, the time during which Micah prophesied

- Neo-Assyrian Empire: major power in the ancient Near East ca. 911–612 BC

- Micah: eighth-century prophet to Judah

- 701 BC: the year that Assyria sieged Jerusalem, along with many other cities in Judah

- Sargon II: Assyrian king who threatened Judah

- An indictment of injustice

- The throne of David to be filled by a deliverer born in Bethlehem

- Right behavior, not manipulating rituals, as the proper response to God's anger

- The coming deliverance from Assyrian threat

Reflection Questions

1. How should Micah 6:8 be applied to the Christian life today?

2. Why do the prophets often include oracles of hope? How should this pattern apply to Christian preaching?

Quiz

1. Micah was a contemporary of the prophet _____.

    a) Jeremiah
    b) Isaiah
    c) Ezekiel
    d) Zephaniah

2. The prophet Micah is specifically referred to in the prophetic book of _____.

    a) Jeremiah
    b) Isaiah
    c) Ezekiel
    d) Zephaniah

3. Which of the following is an Assyrian king who was a threat during Micah's ministry?

    a) Shalmaneser III
    b) Tiglath-Pileser III
    c) Sargon II
    d) Sargon I

4. How many judgment oracles did Micah give?

    a) Three
    b) Four
    c) Five
    d) Seven

5. How many major divisions does Micah have?

    a) Three
    b) Four
    c) Five
    d) Seven

6. Micah ministered during the _____ crisis.

    a) Assyrian
    b) Babylonian

c) Egyptian
d) Judean

7. Each of Micah's major divisions opens with a call to _____.
   a) Argue
   b) Repent
   c) Love
   d) Listen

8. (T/F) Micah's prophecy ends with an oracle of hope.

9. (T/F) Within its context, Micah 6:8 should be understood as a comprehensive statement of God's demands on humanity.

10. (T/F) Micah's message was that the people were guilty of injustice.

ANSWER KEY

1. B, 2. A, 3. C, 4. C, 5. A, 6. A, 7. D, 8. T, 9. F, 10. T

CHAPTER 39

Nahum

You Should Know

- Minor Prophets: known as "The Twelve" in the Hebrew Bible, they are Hosea, Amos, Jonah, Micah, Nahum, Habakkuk, Zephaniah, Obadiah, Joel, Haggai, Zechariah, and Malachi

- Acrostic: a poetic composition in which sets of sequential letters (e.g., initial or final letters of the lines) form a word or phrase or the alphabet

- Oracle: an authoritative prophetic speech

- Nahum: seventh-century prophet of Judah

- Manasseh: king of Judah (695–642 BC) during the ministry of Nahum

- Josiah: king of Judah (640–609 BC) during the ministry of Nahum

- Whereas the people of Nineveh repented when confronted by Jonah, such was not the case with Nahum nearly a century later.

- The impending judgment of Nineveh

- The oracles of judgment were probably addressed as a word of encouragement to the people of Judah.

- Judah's coming release from the power of the Assyrian Empire

Reflection Questions

1. After the fantastic repentance shown in the book of Jonah, why would the prophet Nahum declare judgment on Nineveh?

2. What do the books of Nahum and Jonah teach about repentance and faith in God?

Quiz

1. The book of Nahum opens with an introductory _____.

   a) Lament
   b) Prayer
   c) Psalm
   d) Dirge

2. The book of Nahum contains many parallels to the book of _____ including vocabulary, phrasing, theme, and motif.

   a) Isaiah
   b) Amos
   c) Jonah
   d) Hosea

3. The second section of the book of Nahum contains alternating addresses to Nineveh and _____.

   a) Thebes
   b) Judah
   c) Babylon
   d) Damascus

4. Nahum deals with which ancient Near Eastern empire?

   a) Assyria
   b) Babylon
   c) Egypt
   d) Persia

5. Which nation is the archvillain of the Old Testament?

   a) Assyria
   b) Babylon
   c) Egypt
   d) Persia

6. Which king made Nineveh his capital?

   a) Ashurbanipal
   b) Sargon
   c) Sennacherib
   d) Sargon II

7. Which of the following kings of Judah ruled during the ministry of Nahum?

   a) David
   b) Hezekiah
   c) Josiah
   d) Asa

8. Which other prophet's ministry also involved the city of Nineveh?

   a) Hosea
   b) Amos
   c) Micah
   d) Jonah

9. (T/F) The purpose of the book of Nahum was to pronounce the possibility of Nineveh avoiding destruction through repentance.

10. (T/F) The final section of Nahum contains a dirge suggesting the reasons for God's action against Nineveh.

ANSWER KEY

1. C, 2. A, 3. B, 4. A, 5. A, 6. C, 7. C, 8. D, 9. F, 10. T

CHAPTER 40

Habakkuk

You Should Know

- Minor Prophets: known as "The Twelve" in the Hebrew Bible, they are Hosea, Amos, Jonah, Micah, Nahum, Habakkuk, Zephaniah, Obadiah, Joel, Haggai, Zechariah, and Malachi
- Habakkuk: seventh-century prophet of Judah
- Josiah: king of Judah (640–609 BC) during the ministry of Habakkuk
- Theophany: an audible or visible manifestation of God
- Nabopolassar: led the Chaldean rebellion against Assyria and established the independent Babylonian state
- Babylonian Empire: major power in the ancient Near East ca. 612–539 BC
- God is just in dealing with nations.
- Judah was to receive punishment from the Babylonians, who would in turn be punished by God.
- Even when world events are confusing, we need to trust God and act with integrity.
- God expects more from those who have received more.

Reflection Questions

1. What is God's response to Habakkuk's complaints? Do you think God's response is adequate? Explain.

2. Given that Habakkuk was a contemporary of Jeremiah, what accounts for the differences in their ministries?

Quiz

1. The book of Habakkuk is organized around several _____ by the prophet.

    a) Psalms
    b) Dirges
    c) Inquiries
    d) Monologues

2. The main question of the book of Habakkuk is, _____?

    a) How could God let Jerusalem fall
    b) How can those who are wicked go unpunished
    c) How can Israel survive without a temple
    d) How could God allow King Josiah to die

3. In the book of Habakkuk, the main instrument of God's judgment will be _____.

    a) Plagues
    b) The Babylonians
    c) Drought
    d) The Assyrians

4. Habakkuk deals with God's justice on a/an _____ level.

    a) Individual
    b) Societal
    c) National
    d) Global

5. Habakkuk was a contemporary of which prophet?

    a) Jeremiah
    b) Isaiah
    c) Ezekiel
    d) Nahum

6. Where is the message of the book of Habakkuk found?

    a) In the prophet's questions
    b) In the sins of the people

c) In God's response
d) In the prophet's prayers

7. When did Josiah come to the throne of Judah?
   a) 609 BC
   b) 722 BC
   c) 701 BC
   d) 640 BC

8. (T/F) Habakkuk was concerned with the justice of God at a time when a wicked nation was prospering.

9. (T/F) There is a "wisdom" tone to the prophecy of Habakkuk.

10. (T/F) According to the book of Habakkuk, God is unjust in his dealings with the nations.

ANSWER KEY

1. C, 2. B, 3. B, 4. C, 5. A, 6. C, 7. D, 8. T, 9. T, 10. F

CHAPTER 41

Zephaniah

You Should Know

- Minor Prophets: known as "The Twelve" in the Hebrew Bible, they are Hosea, Amos, Jonah, Micah, Nahum, Habakkuk, Zephaniah, Obadiah, Joel, Haggai, Zechariah, and Malachi
- Zephaniah: seventh-century prophet of Judah
- Theophany: an audible or visible manifestation of God
- Eschatology: that branch of theology concerned with end-time events (i.e., the doctrine of last things)
- Josiah: king of Judah (640–609 BC) during the ministry of Zephaniah
- Babylonian Empire: major power in the ancient Near East ca. 612–539 BC
- The coming day of the Lord
- Numerous "days of the Lord" will precede the final day.
- The call to the humble to seek the Lord
- The universal impact of the coming judgment

Reflection Questions

1. Why did Judah never recover from Manasseh's fifty-year reign of spiritual apostasy? Why were Josiah's spiritual reforms ultimately unsuccessful?

2. According to Zephaniah, what is the Day of the LORD, and what is its significance?

Quiz

1. The prophet Zephaniah was a contemporary of the prophet
   _____.

   a) Jeremiah
   b) Isaiah
   c) Nahum
   d) Amos

2. Who was the pagan nation threatening Judah during the time of Zephaniah's ministry?

   a) Assyria
   b) Babylon
   c) Persia
   d) Aram

3. According to the superscription of the book (1:1), the prophecies of Zephaniah are dated to the reign of _____.

   a) Hezekiah
   b) Josiah
   c) Manasseh
   d) Ahaz

4. Which nation would eventually exile Judah?

   a) Assyria
   b) Egypt
   c) Persia
   d) Babylon

5. Zephaniah and which other OT book are the only Minor Prophets to include oracles against the nations?

   a) Amos
   b) Obadiah
   c) Habakkuk
   d) Malachi

6. What is the most likely date for the prophecy of Zephaniah?

a) 697/696 BC
b) 640/639 BC
c) 627/626 BC
d) 610/609 BC

7. Zephaniah indicted Judah for its corrupt officials and _____.

a) Social injustice
b) Ritualism
c) Keeping of the Sabbath
d) Continued rebellion

8. The apostasy of King _____ for the five decades prior to the ministry of Zephaniah exacted a heavy spiritual toll on Judah.

a) Hezekiah
b) Josiah
c) Manasseh
d) Ahaz

9. (T/F) The purpose of the prophecies by Zephaniah was to initiate change in Judah by pronouncing God's judgment on wickedness.

10. (T/F) Zephaniah's message of judgment for Judah also included a message of eventual restoration.

ANSWER KEY

1. A, 2. B, 3. B, 4. D, 5. A, 6. C, 7. D, 8. C, 9. T, 10. T

CHAPTER 42

Haggai

You Should Know

- Minor Prophets: known as "The Twelve" in the Hebrew Bible, they are Hosea, Amos, Jonah, Micah, Nahum, Habakkuk, Zephaniah, Obadiah, Joel, Haggai, Zechariah, and Malachi
- Haggai: sixth-century prophet of Judah
- Darius I: Persian king who decreed the return of the Judean exiles
- Zerubbabel: governor of Judah who oversaw the rebuilding of the temple
- Chiasm(us): a literary device in which words or phrases parallel one another in reverse order (A-B-C-C-B-A)
- Persian Empire: major power in the ancient Near East ca. 539–332 BC
- The importance of establishing proper priorities.
- The value of the temple as a covenant symbol for Israel.
- The faithfulness of God in renewing his covenant promises to David's descendants.
- The temple would symbolize the covenant presence of Yahweh among his people and mark the Hebrews as God's elect people among the nations.

Reflection Questions

1. In what way had the temple become a "lucky charm" for Judah? Are there evidences of this type of mentality among Christians today?

2. What is the significance of the temple for Christians today?

Quiz

1. Haggai was a contemporary of the other postexilic prophet, _____.

   a) Isaiah
   b) Jeremiah
   c) Obadiah
   d) Zechariah

2. The backdrop for Haggai's prophecy was the reign of _____, king of Persia.

   a) Nebuchedrezzar
   b) Darius I
   c) Xerxes II
   d) Cyrus

3. How many "messages" comprise the book of Haggai?

   a) Three
   b) Four
   c) Five
   d) Six

4. Which books comprise the corpus of Old Testament Prophetic literature dating to the Persian period of Hebrew history (ca. 550–330 BC)?

   a) Zechariah, Daniel, Joel, and Malachi
   b) Jeremiah, Daniel, Amos, and Joel
   c) Jeremiah, Habakkuk, Nahum, and Amos
   d) Isaiah, Nahum, Malachi, and Habakkuk

5. Which of the following led a return of Judean exiles?

   a) Zerubbabel
   b) Zephaniah
   c) Zechariah
   d) Zadok

6. How long did it take to build the first temple?
   a) 10 years
   b) 12 years
   c) 18 years
   d) 7 years

7. Haggai shows literary skill in which of the following ways?
   a) Use of varied phraseology
   b) Use of chiasmus
   c) Wordplay
   d) All of the above

8. (T/F) One of Haggai's concerns was the rebuilding of the walls of Jerusalem.

9. (T/F) Haggai prophesied that God would overthrow the nations and restore Israel's fortunes.

10. (T/F) The fourth address by Haggai promised to establish Zerubbabel as "a signet ring" in Zion, thus rekindling the messianic expectation among the Israelites.

ANSWER KEY

1. D, 2. B, 3. B, 4. A, 5. A, 6. D, 7. D, 8. F, 9. T, 10. T

CHAPTER 43

Zechariah

You Should Know

- Minor Prophets: known as "The Twelve" in the Hebrew Bible, they are Hosea, Amos, Jonah, Micah, Nahum, Habakkuk, Zephaniah, Obadiah, Joel, Haggai, Zechariah, and Malachi

- Dispensationalism: a theological system that understands God's revelation and redemptive program as a sequential series of distinct stages of development

- Eschatology: that branch of theology concerned with end-time events (i.e., the doctrine of last things)

- Zechariah: sixth-century prophet of Judah

- Darius I: Persian king who decreed the return of the Judean exiles and whose rule Zechariah uses to date his oracles

- Persian Empire: major power in the ancient Near East ca. 539–332 BC

- Repentance and covenant renewal

- Hope rooted in God's sovereignty

- Zechariah's vision of the "day of the LORD" was concerned with social justice for the present, not simply for future restoration.

- Zechariah speaks of the messianic shepherd-king.

Reflection Questions

1. How does Zechariah describe the messiah?

2. In what ways does Zechariah impact our understanding of Old Testament eschatology?

Quiz

1. Along with being a prophet, Zechariah was also a _____.

    a) Governmental official
    b) Scribe
    c) Priest
    d) Farmer

2. Zechariah means "_____."

    a) Yahweh is strong
    b) Yahweh has remembered
    c) Yahweh will return
    d) Yahweh is here

3. Zechariah and _____ both encouraged the building of the temple.

    a) Haggai
    b) Malachi
    c) Zephaniah
    d) Isaiah

4. The first section of Zechariah contains _____ "night visions."

    a) Three
    b) Five
    c) Seven
    d) Nine

5. The reign of _____, king of Persia, is the background for Zechariah's prophecies.

    a) Cyrus
    b) Darius I
    c) Xerxes II
    d) Nabonidus

6. Zechariah is often classified as _____ literature.

   a) Wisdom
   b) Proto-apocalyptic
   c) Apocalyptic
   d) Eschatological

7. One of Zechariah's two explicitly stated duties as God's spokesman was to _____ the people of Judah.

   a) Condemn
   b) Comfort
   c) Terrify
   d) Judge

8. T/F Critical scholarship divides Zechariah into five parts on the basis of perceived differences in style, vocabulary, theme, and genre.

9. T/F Zechariah summoned the community to repentance and spiritual renewal.

10. T/F Zechariah has very little to say about the messiah.

ANSWER KEY

1. C, 2. B, 3. A, 4. C, 5. B, 6. B, 7. B, 8. F, 9. T, 10. F

CHAPTER 44

Malachi

You Should Know

- Iconography: pictorial materials (especially conventional images and symbols) associated with a subject (often connected with kingship and religion in the ANE)
- Satrapy: a large administrative district or territory of the Persian Empire ruled by a governor called a "satrap"
- Malachi: sixth-century prophet of Judah whose name means "my angel" or "my messenger"
- Persian Empire: major power in the ancient Near East ca. 539–332 BC
- Great Synagogue: a council of scribes and other Hebrew leaders reputedly founded after the Babylonian exile to reorganize Jewish religious life and culture
- God desires wholehearted worship.
- God expects faithfulness in marriage.
- God hates divorce.
- The "Day of the LORD" affects both the righteous and the wicked.
- An Elijah-like figure will announce the Day of the LORD.

Reflection Questions

1. In what ways does Malachi rely on the Mosaic covenant?

2. How does Malachi inform the Old Testament view of the afterlife? In what way is it consistent with the New Testament view of the afterlife?

Quiz

1. One of the major themes identified in Malachi is _____.
   a) Temple and liturgy
   b) Marriage and divorce
   c) King and land
   d) Judgment of the nations

2. Forty-seven of the fifty-five verses of the book of Malachi address Israel in the _____ person.
   a) First
   b) Second
   c) Third
   d) None of the above; Malachi is addressed specifically to Zerubbabel

3. Malachi is composed of a series of _____ oracles.
   a) Four
   b) Five
   c) Six
   d) Seven

4. Malachi's message is reminiscent of the _____ prophets.
   a) Exilic
   b) Preexilic
   c) Preclassical
   d) Postexilic

5. The people in Malachi ask how they have _____ God.
   a) Served
   b) Loved
   c) Robbed
   d) Angered

6. The returned exiles had difficulties with the _____.
   a) Persians
   b) Egyptians
   c) Samaritans
   d) Philistines

7. Which covenant did Malachi cite specifically?
   a) Covenant of Levi
   b) Covenant of the fathers
   c) Covenant of marriage
   d) All of the above

8. (T/F) Malachi speaks out against idolatry, social injustice, and easy divorce.

9. (T/F) The predominant theme of Malachi is Israel's covenant relationship with God and its ramifications.

10. (T/F) The message of Malachi reflects conditions associated with pre-Ezra decline.

ANSWER KEY

1. B, 2. A, 3. C, 4. B, 5. C, 6. C, 7. D, 8. T, 9. T, 10. T

CHAPTER 45

What We Have Learned

You Should Know

- Transcendence: theologically, the notion of God's "otherness," his distinctness and uniqueness from the created order, his mysterious and unknowable nature

- Monotheism: the view that there is only one God

- Covenant: a contract or treaty that establishes a relationship between two parties

- Covenant theology: a theological system that understands God's relationship to humanity as a divinely established compact or covenant based on the analogy of the interrelationship of the three persons of the Trinity

- The Fall: Adam's and Eve's disobedience in the garden of Eden that introduced sin into the world

- Mount Sinai: mountain where God established the Mosaic covenant

- The Old Testament demonstrates several key attributes of God.

- The contrast between the Old and New Testaments is often painted much too simplistically.

- The presence of God is the central theme of the Bible.

- The Old Testament leaves its readers with hope for the future.

Reflection Questions

1. *Attributes:* Choose three of the attributes listed below which describe an element of God's character or action as presented in the Old Testament. Identify one or two verses from the Old Testament for each of the attributes and discuss the significance of this attribute both for Israel in the Old Testament and for us presently. (Attributes: Creator, Wise, Only God, Transcendent, Righteous and Just, Compassionate and Gracious, Covenant-Making God, Loyal, Redeemer).

2. Choose one of the two false dichotomies described in the section (*Judge vs. Savior*, *Law vs. Grace*); describe why this dichotomy exists, and using two relevant Old Testament texts offer a suggestion as to why this is in fact a false dichotomy.

3. What do the authors identify as a possible *central theme* of the Old Testament? Discuss whether you think this is a good or bad suggestion and why.

CHAPTER 46

Responding to God

You Should Know

- Covenant: a contract or treaty that establishes a relationship between two parties
- Mount Sinai: mountain where God established the Mosaic covenant
- Deuteronomy: foundational book for the Old Testament "law of love"
- Libation: drink offering for a deity
- Repentance: a turning away from sin and a forsaking of all evil and wickedness
- Obedience: the faithful keeping of God's commands, which flows out of a love for God
- The law of love governed people's relationship with God in the Old Testament.
- Worship in the Old Testament differed significantly from worship in the wider ANE culture.
- Worship in the Old Testament is predicated on the people's relationship with God.
- God's plan for his people from the beginning was that they would live justly and rightly.

Reflection Questions

1. Describe the basis for "The Old Testament as the Law of Love." List at least one verse which pertains to this discussion.

2. Describe how the peoples of the ancient Near East understood worship.

3. Tell how God's description of himself contrasted sharply with the prevailing understanding of worship in the ancient Near East.

4. Discuss the idea of worship as a response to God's deeds. Give one example from Scripture.

5. Discuss the connection of social action to worship in the Old Testament. Give at least one relevant example from Scripture which talks about this idea.

CHAPTER 47

The Journey to Jesus

You Should Know

- Covenant: a contract or treaty that establishes a relationship between two parties

- Mount Sinai: mountain where God established the Mosaic covenant

- Covenant land: the land of Israel, which God promised to the children of Abraham as part of his covenant

- Messiah (Heb. "anointed one"): Generally one set apart for a divinely appointed office, such as a priest or a king. Specifically, the title identifies a figure prominent in Old Testament prophetic writings who serves as Israel's deliverer-king (realized in Jesus of Nazareth according to the New Testament writers).

- Old Covenant: the Mosaic covenant enacted at Mount Sinai

- New Covenant: the covenant inaugurated with the birth, life, death, and resurrection of Jesus Christ

- Several themes bridge the two testaments: salvation, covenant, knowledge of God, and the land of covenant promise.

- Jesus is the goal of the Old Testament.

- The New Testament makes extensive use of the Old Testament through quotations and allusions.

- Though the new covenant has already been instituted, the church awaits its final consummation with the return of Christ.

Reflection Questions

1. The authors identify three major headings of the New Testament references to the Old Testament: (1) those related to God Almighty, (2) those related to Jesus as the Christ, and (3) those related to humankind. Please choose two of these three major headings and identify a place in the New Testament where there is reference to the Old Testament. Discuss the relationship of these two texts.

2. Another useful model for bridging the Old and New Testaments is tracing the theme of covenant specifically in relation to (1) salvation or deliverance, (2) the covenant community, (3) the knowledge of God, and (4) the land of covenant promises. Choose two of these dimensions of covenant and describe how that specific dimension helps to form a bridge between the Old and New Testaments.

Notes

www.ingramcontent.com/pod-product-compliance
Lightning Source LLC
LaVergne TN
LVHW030634080426
835508LV00023B/3359